SOS NICARAGUA

ANTHOLOGY BY
EVAN DAUS

Short Stories by Evan Daus, Aidin Lobo Silvestre, Sacuanjoche, Fernando Ortiz, H. Hoffman, Roberto Carlos Pérez, Ryan W. N., and Carlos Luna.

Editing by Becky Hayes, Evan Daus, Max Rose and Ryan W. N..

Translation by Evan Daus.

Cover Art by Aurelio Rodriguez.

The names of some authors and individuals mentioned in their stories have been changed for their safety.

All of these stories are based on true events in Nicaragua. Although certain characters and aspects of the stories have been added for literary effect, the anthologist has been careful to accurately represent the atrocities and politics of the Nicaraguan crisis.

ISBN: 9781790303489

DEDICATION

This book is dedicated to José Abraham Amador and the hundreds of other people killed by state sponsored brutality in Nicaragua. You deserved much better. It is heartbreaking that your life was cut so short.

CONTENTS

ACKNOWLEDGMENTS

This book is the product of an outstanding community effort. No one person could properly convey the diverse experiences chronicled here. I am especially indebted to my coauthors: Aidin Lobo Silvestre, Sacuanjoche, Fernando Ortiz, H. Hoffman, Roberto Carlos Pérez, Ryan W. N., and Carlos Luna. Through your beautiful and heartfelt writing the world will gain a greater understanding of Nicaraguan life and the country's current humanitarian crisis. I am also extremely grateful for Becky Hayes, Ryan W. N. and Max Rose, my talented copy editors; your help was invaluable to the creation of this anthology. Last but certainly not least, I am extremely thankful for Aurelio Rodriguez who created the beautiful cover art for this book.

FOREWORD

This anthology is separated into two parts: culture and crisis. I feel that it is necessary to first introduce the beautiful, altruistic, pious and vibrant aspects of Nicaraguan culture before delving into the current humanitarian crisis.

It is my hope that this book will help readers understand Nicaraguan culture, humanize the victims of the current crisis, and bear witness to the atrocities committed by the Nicaraguan government.

PART ONE: CULTURE

DECEMBER
AIDIN LOBO SILVESTRE
MANAGUA

When a foreigner asks me the best time of year to visit Nicaragua, I always tell them that it is the month of December—without doubt.

December is my favorite month for a thousand reasons. Each time that December arrives, it feels like I am reborn, and I remember so many wonderful moments in my life. It is like reliving the past, without abandoning the present. I live every December with passion; I wish those days would last forever.

My first memory of December was a peculiar one. I was four years old and I remember it as if it were yesterday. It was in 1972, a catastrophic year for Nicaragua—an earthquake ravaged Managua, the city where I was born. On the night of December 22 at around midnight, Managua experienced this traumatic episode.

It was painful to see people crying, frantically running from place to place, wholly consumed by the fear and darkness of the night. I remember the dust from the destruction: crumbled buildings, homes, walls, roofs. Although it was difficult for everyone, at the tender age of four, it was a transcendental experience—but not due to the feeling of the shaking earth and the despair of the unknown. It was transcendental because of what it meant. It was my first experience with nature, and I was fully aware of what was happening around me. I remember being quite happy. I enjoyed the beautiful full moon, and sleeping while exposed to the elements. I thought I was camping, and I was elated to contemplate and experience such natural beauty.

Our family spent the next few days living with our neighbors in an empty lot, as it was unsafe to return to the rubble that remained where our houses once stood. My family decided to take refuge in the nearby hamlet of Las Maderas, which pertains to the municipality of Tipitapa. It was a rural place where my grandfather owned a ranch. Everything was novel, otherworldly: mountains, paved roads, wells for extracting clean water, beautiful rivers and lush trees, clean air, and barnyard animals. There were horses, cows, pigs and goats, as well as less pleasant creatures, such as scorpions and snakes. It felt like I had traveled to a foreign country. Ever since then, I have had a deep interest in country life; experiencing it feels like going on vacation, dreamlike.

I had begun a new adventure in my life, and even at that young age, I paid attention to the differences between urban and rural life. I learned many new things: how to bathe and wash laundry in the river, how to catch fish using my hands, how to milk cows and herd livestock, how to butcher a pig, how to ride a horse, how to sleep in hammocks in the hallway of the house while listening to the sound of insects, how to use a latrine, how to eat *cuajada*[1] with fresh tortillas. These "firsts" excited me, and throughout my three months in Las Maderas, I felt like my eyes were being opened to the wider world.

After this age of discovery, everything started to change for me. I gained a deeper interest in people: their economic, social, cultural and religious activities, and December is by far the best time of year to observe and experience these activities. Although Nicaragua has many holidays throughout the year, both local and national in scale, December feels like a month packed with holidays and celebrations. *La Gritería* is my favorite holiday, and it falls on the 7th of December each year, after nine days of prayer. *La Gritería* originated as a catholic holiday, but nowadays the celebration is shared by people of many faiths. For the majority of Nicaraguans, it is the most anticipated holiday.

During the nine days of prayer preceding *La Gritería*, family members and friends meet to pray and sing to the Virgin. These days are always filled with joy. The songs and the gifts of fruits, sweets and other specialties create a happy environment that continues to build over the course

---

[1] A cheese product, typical of rural Nicaragua.

of the nine days. *La Gritería* is a time for sharing and giving back to the wider community. The final day is the most special of all. At around six or seven in the evening, people light fireworks to initiate the celebration. Children and adults alike walk the streets with bags in hand, singing at the altars that have been erected by their neighbors, eagerly anticipating the candy and gifts that they will receive in return for their serenades. The cities of León, Granada and Managua are especially famous for their vibrant celebrations of *La Gritería.*

The neighborhood where I was born and raised, Monseñor Lezcano in west Managua, tries to outshine all of the other parts of the city in its festivities. In this old neighborhood, people perform daily religious marches at four in the morning, on each of the nine days of prayer. These marches are jubilant occasions, complete with fireworks and the deafeningly loud sounds of the *chichera* bands playing Nicaraguan music. Everyone participates in these marches, and they are among the most popular events in Managua.

Although this religious celebration typically comes at the beginning of the month, there are some Nicaraguans who observe the nine days of prayer and the celebration of the Virgin throughout all of December. This is usually the case when they are unable to observe the stipulated dates, but feel compelled to complete this celebration, as they consider it a promise to God.

During much of my adolescence, I participated in these ceremonies in both the neighborhood where I lived and in my grandmother's neighborhood. Although I was never a talented singer, people would happily participate in the prayers that I led. In these celebrations, the voice of the singer does not matter, only their will to praise the beloved Virgin and the Immaculate Conception. I was inspired by my mother, who organized the community prayers for our block. She charged me with going to each house on our street to pray with our neighbors' guests. I followed in my mother's footsteps, and I continue to participate and organize these celebrations to this day. These religious traditions are ingrained in Nicaraguan culture and form an important part of our identity.

After these lively celebrations, we begin the preparations for Christmas, another important holiday for both rich and poor Nicaraguans. Although each families' celebrations differ based on their finances, the holiday is universally merry and has a unique *Nica* touch.

As soon as the nine days of prayer and *La Gritería* are over, every market, shopping center and radio station in Nicaragua starts playing Christmas music. These melodies fill us with joy and transport us back to our childhoods at the speed of light.

Starting on the 16th of December, nativity scenes begin to pop up in Masaya, Granada, Managua and other towns. Many churches reenact the journey of Joseph and Mary, using children dressed in their likenesses. On each of these mornings, costumed children travel to a different house, where they beseech the owners for shelter. Each of the homeowners denies the children entrance, simulating the story of Joseph and Mary in Bethlehem. After the children sing Christmas carols for the adults of the home, the doors open for the children and the owner offers a toast to the young guests. This reenactment repeats for nine days, culminating on December 24th, when the final homeowner hosts a large celebration for the children, giving them sweets, toys, and full breakfasts.

This tradition is very common at my neighborhood church, and every year I am transported back to my childhood, reliving the nine day celebration of the Holy Child. My grandmother, brothers, cousins and I would sing the Christmas songs and play the tambourine and the *chichiles*[2] to give rhythm to the carols. Though I never loved waking up early, I refused to miss this beautiful celebration. I remember being enchanted by the starry sky and crisp air of the early morning, which left me shivering cold. These early mornings in December were special because they were the only time of year that we could enjoy cold weather and wear sweaters. In addition to the cold, there was sometimes a light drizzle or breeze, which we considered a blessing and called "the urine of the Holy Child." It was exhilarating to see the sunrise as we made our religious procession; I was captivated as the darkness died and made way for the light of day as we returned home and shared a big, warm breakfast made by my aunt.

Finally, the most anticipated day of the month arrives. Christmas is celebrated in all of Nicaragua, and we truly make the most of it. Sadly, in our country, like many Latin

---

[2] An Nicaraguan take on maracas, weaved together with palm leaves.

American countries, there exists a marked difference between those who have a lot and those who have nothing. But when it comes to this celebration, that difference does not matter. Each person celebrates within their means, and the most important part of the holiday is to celebrate the birth of the Jesus Christ and his reason for coming to Earth. Focusing on this makes us forget our economic differences.

In Nicaragua, Christmas is a time for family. On the 24th, most families gather for a special dinner at midnight. Many people make *nacatamales*[3], which are both delicious and very affordable. Another Nicaraguan favorite is stuffed hen, and some Nicaraguan families opt for the luxury of a pig's leg or beef tenderloin, as well as traditional desserts such as *buñuelos*[4] or *sopa borracha*[5].

It is customary to show off a new outfit on Christmas day, though if a person cannot afford a completely new outfit, a new shirt or shoes will suffice.

In some families that maintain the myth of Santa Claus, they send the kids to bed early, only to awaken them at midnight to spoil them with gifts. Nicaraguans love fireworks, and Christmas is definitely no exception. These festive explosions are constant on Christmas day, and much of the holiday season.

---

[3] Similar to a tamal. In this dish, corn dough is filled with meat, vegetables and spices, then wrapped in a banana leaf, and boiled.

[4] Nicaraguan *buñuelos* consist of yuca and cheese dough, fried and served with honey.

[5] Rum cake.

Another tradition is the "Christmas hug," in which everyone embraces each other: families, neighbors, friends, couples. In many cases, the hug is a moment of reconciliation between people with personal differences.

Of course, there are variations in all of these customs, such as the tradition of the Christmas soup made by the Nicaraguan Creoles of Bluefields. After attending Christmas mass, they open their homes and doors to the public, and invite anyone to come in and share the soup that they prepared for the occasion.

In my family, our celebration of the holidays has changed over the years. When I was a young girl, all of my family members would gather at my grandmother's home, where we would stay up late and eat whatever we wanted, while waiting to open our gifts and watch the effervescent fireworks. As time passed, each family went their own way for the holidays. For a few years, we went to our aunt's house for Christmas; later we celebrated at my mother's house until she finally left this world. Nowadays, our immediate family continues to spend the holidays with my aunts, reminiscing about how we used to play as kids, and trying to recreate that experience for our children.

After Christmas, we get ready to send off the old year and happily receive the new one. A tradition for the New Year is the "burning of the old year." Some people create dolls using old clothing stuffed with paper and gunpowder, which they hang from tree branches and street posts. At the stroke of midnight, they burn the dolls, and watch as their representation of the old year burns, explodes and disappears.

Similarly to Christmas, a generous dinner is prepared and is typically eaten after midnight—honoring the first hours of the new year. Each family or group of friends gives thanks to both God and their ancestors, for having completed another year of life, eagerly ushering in the new one. At the dinner table, we lay out an extra plate, to represent the members of our family who are no longer with us, and we leave it full of food so that they too can eat.

In addition to the burning dolls, the streets are full of fireworks, and the happiness is palpable and contagious. People greet one another, visit their neighbors' homes, and party together until the early morning.

The final festivity of this season is the Feast of the Wise Men. Although it is smaller than the other holidays of the Christmas season, it is not to be overlooked. This simple and religious holiday has a special place in my heart, because my little daughter was born on the eve of the feast, and was given the name Estefanía, a derivative of the word *epifanía*, meaning epiphany— an apparition, manifestation or phenomenon. In the religious sense, the feast celebrates the divine manifestation of the arrival of the Wise Men, who brought gifts and worshiped the Holy Child. "Epiphany" can also be defined in the philosophical sense, as a profound feeling of realization or understanding. An epiphany is something felt in the heart, and it is the feeling that something that was once difficult to comprehend or achieve is now and forevermore solved, completed, or understood. All of these meanings represent how I feel for my little *nena*; she is a gift from God and the

Wise Men. Before she was born, I thought I was unable to have more children, and so she is a manifestation of how one must never lose hope. Estefanía is my profound sense of self-realization as a mother.

Personally, I have never celebrated any of these holidays away from my family, so I cannot say how they are celebrated in other places, or with other people; though I imagine that they must share the same sentiment and warmth.

The value of these holidays goes beyond tradition; they are laden with memories and details of my life which are impossible to forget. Among these are a few sad memories of the loved ones we have lost, but most of them are joyous and wholesome. We share these holidays with our children and teach them of their importance, in the hope that they keep these traditions alive. Each year I anxiously await the arrival of December, to spend my vacation days organizing the many celebrations, and practicing and sharing the message of our Lord Jesus Christ: love for our fellow man.

LIFE AND CUSTOMS OF A
NICARAGUAN BARRIO
SACUANJOCHE
MANAGUA

Daily Life in the *Barrios*

As a young girl, I grew up in a humble home in a *barrio*[6] of Managua. My childhood was happy and calm; my family and neighbors were all modest people, but each of them had an enormous, caring heart. I think about those days often.

From my bedroom window, I enjoyed the aroma of vines that occasionally flowered, releasing a profusion of jasmine smells, while my cousins played and joked on the patio. We would listen to the melody of the birds that regaled us with their trills just before the sun flirted its first rays

---

[6] A neighborhood or district of a town in a Spanish-speaking country.

through the leaves of the pink mango, guava, icaco and orange trees that populated the courtyard of our house.

Our home, like many Nicaraguan homes, had a central patio filled with trees that nourished us with fruit and protected us from the merciless tropical sun. You can visit any house in the old *barrios* of Managua and at the end of your visit, the host will give you mangos, miniature bananas, nísperos, or guavas, depending on the size of the yard and the host's enthusiasm to plant and care for their trees.

The adults in my family would sit and chat in the central patio, while the children would run around and play on the sidewalks and narrow alleys in the surroundings of my house. We would kick around soccer balls—dreaming of becoming famous and playing in the World Cup.

Sunday mornings were always a special time for my family. On these days, we would have a delicious breakfast consisting of bread, coffee and a fresh *nacatamal*. At lunchtime, it was normal to look for a neighbor who had already prepared a succulent dish for lunch, since nobody wanted to cook on Sundays. If we had any money, we would opt to buy lunch from one of our more culinarily inclined neighbors. Finding these homes was easy; we walked around the *barrio* in search of a house with a sign saying "We've got *vaho*[7]," "We've got *carne asada*[8]," or "*Sopa de res*[9]."

In my house, we ate *sopa de res* religiously every Monday. We were ten children and seven adults in the household, and for that reason we cooked the soup in a gigantic cauldron. In addition to the *sopa de res* with a variety of vegetables cooked into it, the meal was served with shredded beef, rice, and boiled sweet plantains. I never fully understood why we held this tradition, but I sometimes think it was to energize the body for the week of hard work that was just beginning.

Barrio Solidarity

The solidarity of Nicaraguan *barrios* has always inspired me, especially in the older, more traditional *barrios*. If a family is having financial problems, many of their neighbors will become invested in their wellbeing and try to help them. This is especially true in the case of elderly individuals and single mothers. Support may be in the form of food, clothing, medicine or work opportunities.

In my *barrio*, there was one case that I remember vividly and have reflected upon often. There was a octogenarian woman living with her wheelchair-bound daughter, and neither of them could work due to their precarious health. However, they never went without. Every neighbor on the

---

[7] Beef, yuca, and green plantains mixed together and served on a banana leaf.

[8] Barbecued beef.

[9] Beef soup.

block and many from the surrounding area, including my grandmother, would provide them with food and medicine. A nearby doctor also helped, donating his time and expertise. Both women lived in simple conditions, but they always received visitors with great warmth, sincerity, and appreciative smiles. Although they had few material possessions, they lived happy and grateful lives with their neighbors and community members.

In the Catholic churches of most *barrios*, there are special groups who collect food, sanitary products, medicine and financial donations from their members each month. These are then distributed to the elderly, sick and financially disadvantaged individuals from the surrounding area.

In the case of sick individuals, it is common for neighbors to inquire about their health, and ask what foods they need for a quick recovery. For diabetic individuals, neighbors will often visit and bring bouquets of Jamaica flowers (known in other countries as hibiscus), which can be made into a sugarless tea. When someone catches the flu, neighbors will often prepare them medicinal teas (made from the herbs in their gardens), or chicken soup. For any other minor health problem, the neighbors might bring over gifts of fruits, fresh squeezed juices or cookies. Visiting the homes of sick people is routine for all Nicaraguans, but especially the elderly. My grandmother says that this is because the elderly are always concerned about the wellbeing of their friends and neighbors.

Barrio solidarity is particularly important when a community member passes away. Close neighbors accompany the grieving family to the wake and funeral, supporting them with gifts of coffee, cake and bread. In the older and more traditional *barrios*, such as mine, they hire a truck with loudspeakers to circle the streets and disseminate the mournful announcement. Don't be alarmed if you are having dinner at your home and suddenly hear a voice through a loudspeaker announcing the death of "Sutanito" who was commonly known as "*el chele*," and providing the date, time and location of the wake and the funeral.

The community members continue to support the grieving families through the nine days of prayer which proceed the funeral. On the ninth day of mourning, those present pray the Rosary and share food and drink with the family of the deceased. On these occasions, most families serve *chilate,* a drink made from purple corn, milk and spices. In the small towns outside of Managua, the families go even further— preparing lavish feasts for the occasion and sacrificing cows and chickens to make a variety of delicacies for their guests.

A Few Urban Legends

Part of Nicaraguan folklore is telling scary stories of apparitions and inexplicable events. These stories vary from town to town, and many people accept them as fact.

In my *barrio*, we tell a story of the Devil who appears on the main avenue after midnight. He appears in the form of a horseman with an indistinguishable face mounted on a pitch black steed with blood red eyes. A few of the women who live on the main avenue say that on sleepless nights, they hear the violently loud and fast-paced approach of a horse. When they look out the front window, they all see the black horse but none of them have been able to see the face of the rider. The horseman rides through town, almost arriving at the church but never venturing in front of it, then he returns from whence he came.

Another story that my mother told me, was about the town drunk, who would get drunk every day and abuse his children physically and psychologically with all kinds of insults. One day, an unknown force lifted him into the air and his screams for help were heard throughout the *barrio*. He was on his knees, but without anyone or anything touching him, he levitated a few centimeters up from the ground. Because his screams were heart wrenching and because it was daytime, the curious neighbors came out of their houses to see what had happened to the poor man. They were astonished to find the man levitating above the ground, controlled by some mysterious and invisible force. Horrified, the neighbors ran to find the town priest, asking him for prayers and a divine intercession to help the poor drunkard's tormented soul.

My mom told me that the priest rushed to the scene and stood by the possessed man. The priest prayed and prayed, while sprinkling the man with holy water, but the priest's prayers were inaudible to those present at the scene. The man became insane and enraged every time the holy water touched his skin. The priest hurriedly walked with the man in this way for five blocks, until the possessed man finally fell to the ground, emitting a deafening roar and fainting. When he finally awoke, he was stunned, and asked what had happened.

Traditions that Live in Our Hearts

Despite the enticing technology and novelties that have arrived in Nicaragua over the past few decades, we refuse to abandon the traditions and customs described here. Some of us continue these traditions because it was the way of our grandparents; others choose to keep the traditions alive because of our Nicaraguan pride. In either case, these traditions are so ingrained in our hearts that we keep them alive as part of our identity.

To live in a Nicaraguan *barrio* is something beautiful and gratifying—our community nourishes the soul, inspires the spirit and captivates the heart.

It nourishes the soul because we share with those on our block: our happiness, our sadness, and our turns of fate. It inspires the spirit because each home inspires self-reflection and teaches us a new lesson. The *barrio* is so dear to our hearts, that always; always our thoughts will return to the place that we love and that we call home.

ALONE IN MASAYA
FERNANDO ORTIZ
MASAYA

It was the Saturday before Mother's Day 2017 and I still didn't have a gift for my host mother. She had been taking care of me for the past three months. As a Peace Corps Trainee, I had been placed in a home with a local Nicaraguan family. The purpose of the homestay is to participate in local traditions, customs and simply learn by watching their day to day life— which can sometimes be very different from our daily lives in the US.

My host family has been hosting Peace Corps Trainees for a long time, and they are highly regarded within the Peace Corps community. They have hosted eight trainees, four women and four men, including myself. After three months of living with my host mother, Mama Liliam, I figured out the perfect gift for her. Every time I entered Mama Liliam's house, I noticed that she had an assortment of printed photos. One of the first things I learned about Nicaraguan culture is that they truly value printed photos, especially those of their loved ones. My host mother proudly keeps a photo of every female trainee she has hosted, however there were none of the male trainees. After doing some investigating, I found out that none of them had gone out of their way to print one. So, I thought that the best gift I could give her was a picture of the two of us together.

I decided to go on an adventure to the nearby city of Masaya to print the photos. For me, this trip was huge—I had never gone to Masaya by myself. I didn't know much about the city, let alone where to find a printing store. My only thought was to go to the center of the city. After taking the correct bus to Masaya from the small town of Masatepe, I got off at the Masaya Market, a sprawling commercial center with hundreds of merchants which also serves as a major bus terminal. Any person can tell you that the Masaya Market is its own little world and getting out of it on foot can be a confusing feat, though it has only one entrance and one exit for automotives and buses. Seeing the exiting vehicles, I decided to follow them—it wasn't the fastest route but it was the easiest one. The path lead me to the outskirts of the market, where there are hundreds of other merchants and stores. Once out of the madness of vendors and buses, my real mission began: finding a printing store in the labyrinth of this unfamiliar city.

Most of the locals whom I asked told me that the stores had gone out of business. After asking a few more people,

I began heading to the center of the city to try my luck. I was easily one kilometer away from the city center when I stopped, waiting to cross one of the dozens of streets that separate Masaya's center from its market, when I saw an old woman in her late sixties—I had a feeling that she would know where to direct me.

I crossed the street and asked her if she knew of any printing shops. She answered that the shop was far away, but that she would walk me there. It didn't matter that I told her that it wasn't necessary or that I didn't want to occupy her time. She was as insistent as she was kind, two qualities which seem ubiquitous in older Nicaraguan *señoras*.

We began walking downtown and as we chatted she quickly realized that I have another Spanish accent. Our conversation proceeded the way it usually does, introducing myself and answering her questions: *Where are you from? What are you doing in Nicaragua?* After explaining my Puerto Rican heritage and my work with the Peace Corps, she told me that her name was Doña Teresa, and that she is from Masaya.

It took us 10 minutes to get to the printing store and to our surprise, the store didn't have electricity, so we were told to come back later. Outside of the store we continued talking, and I, being grateful for her help, offered to help her finish her errands. We walked to the pharmacy at the other corner of the plaza to pick up her prescriptions, we talked about our families and I told her about a friend of mine who was going to live in Masaya.

I've been traveling for four years, and these experiences have helped me develop a good sense of listening and an ability to make friends easily. This was one of those occasions where I could sense a very kind soul and I was elated to be able to keep her company that day. After the pharmacy, she wanted to buy flowers for a saint at her church, located in the middle of the plaza. We picked out a beautiful bouquet and our conversation continued to flow naturally like we had known each other for years. We got to the church and Doña Teresa began to pray in front of the chapel and while she was doing that I took a picture of her. She obviously loved this, because as soon as Teresa finished praying she began to pose for a few more photos in front of the chapel. After she was satisfied with her impromptu photoshoot, we headed back to the printing store which finally had electricity.

In addition to the photos of my host mother, I decided to print the photos that I had just taken of Teresa to show my appreciation for her help. I finished in the shop and I went to the bench where Teresa was waiting and I gave her the pictures of her at the church. She was ecstatic, her face lit up with pure delight. My new friend was taken aback by this simple act that would be considered normal in my culture. This experience with Doña Teresa shows the nature of most Nicaraguans. They are humble, open people who are willing to help strangers without expecting anything in return, but they are thrilled and appreciative of small, thoughtful gestures, like the gift of a photo.

PART TWO: CRISIS

MY EVACUATION
EVAN DAUS
MASAYA

I didn't ever think this could happen. At least not like this.

Social security reforms?

It seems like the type of thing that people would debate and get angry about, but not the type of thing that would lead the country to the brink of a civil war.

In the days leading up to the outbreak of violence, I heard mentions of proposed reforms to the Nicaraguan social security system, and I knew that people were upset. But people were always upset about something in politics, and I assumed that this would just fade away from the public attention like things usually do.

It was on the 18th of April, 2018 when the reforms were signed into law.

When I first heard the news, I didn't think much of it. I was sitting at the bar of the Laguna Beach Club with my good friends Carlos and Gary, who manage the establishment. The beach club is a beautiful lakefront hotel on the Laguna de Apoyo, a pristine crater lake in southern Nicaragua.

I had stopped by the hotel to have lunch on my way to a high school in that community, where I teach entrepreneurship classes.

"Wow it really happened," said Gary, showing us a headline on his phone. "Ortega signed the social security reforms into law. It's official."

"What does that mean?" I asked. "I know it involves cutting pensions, but who will be affected?"

"It affects everyone," he replied. "The changes to the social security system cut the pensions for all retired people in Nicaragua, and it will raise the level of taxation on everyone who is working."

"It even affects us," added Carlos. "When we retire in a few decades, our pensions will be reduced at an even greater rate than the people who are retired now."

"What prompted these changes?"

"The current social security system is bankrupt," Carlos continued. "People are upset because Ortega has invested much of the public funds in the businesses of his friends and family. People also believe that he has used the public funds to buy expensive properties which are registered to an anonymous owner."

As Carlos explained these details, he looked unsurprised, but Gary seemed alarmed that the reforms were actually signed into law.

Looking back at his phone, Gary said, "People are very upset about these changes. There are protests planned tomorrow in Managua, Masaya and Leon."

"Wow that is crazy," I mentioned, while turning my attention to my meal.

The conversation moved on to other topics, and I didn't think that the impact of this headline would be different than the other shocking Nicaraguan headlines that I had seen over the years. The government had taken similarly unpopular actions before, but the public's reaction was usually moderate and ephemeral. This news didn't feel any different… at the time.

After another hour of chatting and laughing with my friends, they called a taxi to take me to the high school. As I waited, I went through my backpack to make sure that I had all of the books and materials that I needed for the class I was about to teach at the high school in the Valley of the Laguna.

Upon my arrival at the school, I sought out my Nicaraguan counterpart, Profe Martin, with whom I co-teach the entrepreneurship classes at this school.

Martin was never formally trained in entrepreneurship or business administration. He normally teaches physical education, but was assigned to teach entrepreneurship several years ago. I helped train him in the entrepreneurship curriculum, and I teach the class alongside him.

I went to greet the principal in his office, but neither he nor his secretary were there. This was normal for the small school. I started walking to our classroom, when I saw Profe Martin acting as the referee to a soccer match out on the field.

I spent several minutes watching the students play on the dusty field before being noticed by Profe Martin, who was busy yelling advice and directions to the players.

When he spotted me, Martin handed the whistle to one of the other students and gave him instructions that I couldn't hear.

Smiling, Martin approached me. "Evan! How have you been this week?"

"I have been great, thank you! How is everything going here in the Valley?"

"Everything is fine, thank God. But here's the thing—we are understaffed today and so the entrepreneurship class has been cancelled. I tried to call you, but I didn't have credit on my phone. I am so sorry that you had to travel all the way out here from Masaya."

In reality, the Valley of the Laguna is only a 15 or 20 minute taxi ride from Masaya, but people in this rural community avoid making the commute any more often than is necessary.

"It's no problem, Martin. When will the class be next week?"

"I am not sure yet," he replied thoughtfully "We need to hire an additional teacher as soon as possible to actually teach all of the class sections, but we don't know when that will be. I have already talked to the principal and he agrees that the entrepreneurship class is one of the most important, so he is trying to arrange the schedule for next week so that our class isn't affected by the changes."

"That's fine, thank you for already handling that," I said. "I can call you next Tuesday to confirm that the class will be held at the normal time."

Although class cancellations are a common occurrence in Nicaraguan public schools, Profe Martin almost never misses a class and is always focused on keeping the class ahead of schedule.

Glancing back at the soccer game behind us, Martin smiled and said "Perfect, we'll be in contact next week. Take care of yourself, and good luck with your other classes!"

Before leaving the school, I passed by several of my students and I made sure to greet them and ask about their families. Although I teach around five hundred students throughout my six schools, I make sure to remember the names of the ones who participate actively in the class and answer questions. In the case of this school, it is easy to remember many of the students because they all participate in the class and they love to discuss business topics within the context of their rural community.

I suspect that having a PE instructor teach the entrepreneurship curriculum helps give the class an active, exciting energy that is sometimes lost when the class is taught by older, more traditional teachers.

The students greet me on my way out. "Goodbye Profe, *que le vaya bien.*"

This common phrase translates roughly as "good luck," but does not specify what I might need luck to do.

I walked out of the school and down the shaded residential road which runs through the Valley towards the shared taxi stop, then headed home to Masaya.

Later in the evening, I went to the Central Park of Masaya to meet up with some of my friends from the Peace Corps in my region. As we sat at an open air table drinking our smoothies, we discussed the protests which had already begun in a few urban centers throughout the country.

"In Managua, the university students at the UCA and UNAN have already started protesting," advised Alyssa, a friend of mine who works as a teacher in Managua. "People are really angry, and it looks like protests are supposed to start in Masaya tomorrow morning at eight."

"That is really close to the Peace Corps office," responded Crystal, another Peace Corps Volunteer in Masaya. "I wonder if it is going to affect the trainees who are traveling through the capital tomorrow."

For my part, I had completely forgotten about the trainees. The Peace Corps Trainees were new to Nicaragua, and completely unfamiliar with the capital. Most of our training program is spent in small Nicaraguan towns, where everybody knows each other and it is impossible to get lost. Many of them speak only a little Spanish and would not know how to navigate the city of Managua, even if the streets were safe.

"Hmm, we should just be sure to avoid the areas where they are protesting," I said without much concern. "I am sure that Peace Corps staff will be in contact with the trainees and give them detailed instructions."

Crystal looked at her watch. "It is getting late, I should head home. I need to finish up a few things before school tomorrow."

We were done with our drinks, and the owner of the shop was slowly stacking up the plastic patio chairs, preparing to close for the night.

"Okay," I said while standing up. "Be safe tomorrow. This will all blow over in a few days."

I hugged Alyssa and Crystal goodbye, giving each of them a single kiss next to the cheek, as is customary in Nicaragua.

Walking home, I thought of other things— mainly the work that I had planned for the next day. I had to wake up at eight in the morning to meet with Annie Chajin, a fashion designer and entrepreneur whom I was training in finance and inventory management. After my coaching session with her, I had to travel to a rural school to teach and plan future lessons with Profe Juana, another counterpart of mine.

When I arrived home, I was surprised to find the front door unlocked. Usually I would be the last person home at that time of night.

As I stepped through the front door, I saw my host sister Loyda talking with my host mother Milagros.

I could tell that Loyda was angry about the recent social security reforms, which did not surprise me. Loyda has always been politically active, in both her personal and professional life. She was a proud member of an opposition party called the Sandinista Renovation

Movement (MRS), and served as a congresswoman in the Nicaraguan National Assembly for several years before President Daniel Ortega used an executive order to remove all of the congressmen from the MRS party.

I noticed that Loyda was fully dressed, and ready to leave the house.

"*Hola Mama, Hola Loyda.* How are you?"

"Well, not so great," said my host mother, with her slow and melodic accent, which is typical of the older generations of Nicaraguans.

"Have you heard about the changes to the Social Security system?" asked Loyda.

"Well, yes, but what exactly do they entail?"

"The government has cut the social security payments for all current retirees by 5%, but for people like me who will be retiring in the future, that could be a cut of between 10 and 15%," Loyda explained in frustration. "At the same time, they've increased the amount that all employers and workers will have to pay in taxes. This is even worse for freelancers, because their increase in taxes will be higher than for traditional workers."

As Loyda explained these details, I heard a car pull up to the front of our house.

"I have to go now," said Loyda. "My friends and I are going to Managua to join the protesters. The protests here in Masaya are scheduled to start tomorrow morning at 8 am. You really should not leave the house for anything tomorrow."

Loyda leaned in and kissed both Milagros and I on the cheek before walking out of the house and into the car waiting outside.

"I hope the protests stay calm and contained, *mamá*."

"God willing," she replied. "Good night, Evan."

As I got ready for bed and put on a podcast to fall asleep, I was disrupted by a constant stream of text messages from my fellow Peace Corps Volunteers, spreading unconfirmed rumors about the protests which they swore to be true.

I switched my phone to silent, and went to sleep.

The next morning I woke up at eight and slowly started getting ready for my appointment with Annie. I texted her explaining what material we would be covering that day, and confirming the time of our meeting.

As I left my bedroom, I was greeted again by my host sister. "Good morning Loyda, how was last night?"

"It was a mess," she exclaimed. "The police kept using violence to disperse and repress us, but when you flood a nest of fire ants, they will start to swarm. Retired people are one of the most vulnerable parts of our population, how could the government do this to them?"

Loyda sipped her coffee and pulled out her phone.

"Look at what is happening here in Masaya," she said as she leaned over toward me. "The streets leading into and out of the city are both blocked with protesters, and the police are using tear gas to try to disperse them."

The video she showed me was being broadcast on Facebook Live by one of her friends, giving commentary on what was happening in that part of town.

Setting down her coffee and putting away her phone, Loyda continued, "I am going there now to join the protesters. I am bringing them bottled water and cloth to protect their faces from the tear gas."

"Aren't you afraid of going out there?" I asked nervously.

"It is not a matter of fear," she said. "I have to stand up against these changes. Retired people cannot go out and advocate for themselves, so we have to do it for them."

"Well, be safe," I resigned. "Don't put yourself in too much danger."

As Loyda left, I continued getting ready for my day and gathering the books and supplies that I would need for my class and coaching sessions.

At around 9 am, I got a text message from Profe Juana, "Evan, don't come to El Comején today, class has been cancelled due to the scheduled protests."

I replied, "Okay, thank you for letting me know."

This would give me more time to work with Annie on her inventory and cash flow management. Annie was about to open a new retail store off of the Calle de la Calzada in Granada, one of the most expensive and fashionable streets in the country. This was very exciting for both of us, but it would entail a lot of work, and I was grateful to have more time to spend with her that day.

I had fully packed my backpack and put on my shoes when my host mother asked me, "Which part of the city are you headed to?"

"I am going to an appointment near Siete Esquinas, *Mamá*" I told her.

"I just spoke with Loyda, and you won't be able to get there," she replied. "The Central Park and the streets north of it are filled with protesters. Can your appointment wait for an hour or two?"

"Well, maybe," I paused for a moment. "I think Annie is free all day, so I will let her know that I will arrive later on."

After contacting Annie, I decided to start working from home. Although it was inconvenient to have to delay the meeting, I could use the additional time to create a few worksheets that she and I would be using to track cash flow and inventory levels.

Throughout the morning I heard the sounds of protests, but they did not sound all that different to the sounds of celebrations in Nicaragua. People were chanting on loudspeakers, playing loud music, and there was a constant stream of mortars being set off. The sound of these mortars was nearly identical to those of the fireworks which Nicaraguans light on all occasions, or for no occasion at all.

As I was working, the noises began to change. The chanting turned into yelling, and in addition to the sounds of the mortars, there were other, louder explosions.

"Evan, come out here," shouted my host mom from across the house.

I came out of my room and walked towards my mom and my host brother, standing at the front door, looking outward. She turned to me.

"I want you to see this," she said gravely. "I want you understand the reality of this country."

I walked to the front door, and they both stepped aside, giving me a full view of the street.

I looked out onto the cobblestone street where I lived. The street was bright and hot with the sun sitting directly overhead, making every color seem to pop. The only pedestrians were a few dozen lean young men, wearing tee shirts and jeans, and bandanas covering their noses and mouths. Every one of them was carrying a large rock in their hand. I continued scanning the streets and noticed a large patch of the road was covered in dirt, where the cobblestones had been removed. *I guess that is where these guys found their rocks.*

The ground outside of my doorstep was littered with black debris. My host brother, Olinto picked one up and showed it to me. "Rubber bullets," he said.

"Well at least they're not real bullets," I said trying to lighten the situation. I had read news stories about police in many countries using rubber bullets to disperse crowds, so although I was concerned, I was not scared.

"They can still cause serious damage though," said my host mom. "A boy in Managua was hit the eye with one this morning and it completely destroyed his eyeball."

Cued by my mom's explanation, Olinto pulls out his phone and shows me the graphic, bloodied face of the one-eyed boy.

He looks just like one of my students. I thought, staring at the heavy stream of blood flowing down the boy's face in the photo. *Even if he were just unlucky to have been hit in the eye, how could a government choose to attack children and students like this?* I felt sick to my stomach.

"Such brutality," I said while returning my attention to the street and away from the photo. Besides the young men in the street, the only people in sight were my neighbors, gathered in their doorways just like us.

I heard two or three shots, and a cloud of white smoke started forming on the street corner nearby the house. A second later, three police officers in full riot gear sprinted into view, firing their rubber bullets indiscriminately at anyone in the street or even in the doorways of the homes.

Before I could react, my host brother and mom grabbed me by the arms and pulled me inside, while slamming the metal door shut.

"That is enough spectating for now," said my mom, looking concerned.

Without saying anything, I bit my tongue and walked back to my room to continue my work.

Although my fingers kept busy typing, my mind wandered. I couldn't forget the image of the one-eyed boy, and every explosion reminded me that he wouldn't be the only victim today.

At least he's still alive. I noted. *Nobody has been killed in the riots yet, right?*

Worried, I go online to the local and reliable Nicaraguan news site, La Prensa, to read the latest updates about the riot. Although there have been rumors of deaths, nothing has been confirmed. I breathed a sigh of relief and returned to my work.

By one in the afternoon, it was clear to me that I was not going to be able to leave my house that day for any appointment.

I texted Annie, "I am almost done with the worksheets that we were going to go over today, but I am not going to leave my house due to the protests. I will email you the documents and you can look them over, they are pretty self-explanatory."

Throughout the day I kept hearing the explosions and I tried to ignore them. I knew what they were—tear gas, rubber bullets and mortars. I knew that nobody had started using live ammunition, and why would they? If the government were to use live ammunition against peaceful protesters, all hell would break loose.

I filled the afternoon with busy work. I deep cleaned my bedroom and dusted. I sent emails that I had been putting off, and I worked on my next semiannual report, even though it wouldn't be due for another two months.

By 4 pm I was bored and I felt that I had accomplished everything that I could within the tiny room that housed both my bedroom and office. I was laying on my bed refreshing my email again to see if anything new had arrived, when Loyda arrived home and walked past my room.

"Loyda," I called out to her, "how did it go on the northside of town?"

"The fucking government is trying to scare us and use force to repress the protesters, but it is just making us more angry," she said. "The protests are going to go on all night."

I hadn't eaten for most of the day, and I knew that I had nothing appealing for dinner at home.

"If I order a pizza, would you want some, Loyda?"

"Yes, but you should order it soon before sun sets, because the protests are expected to get more violent after dark."

I walked back to my room and pulled up the phone number of Pizza Hut, and press the call button. Although it isn't considered gourmet fare in the United States, Pizza Hut is a luxury service in Nicaragua, and is priced accordingly.

After two rings, the call connected. "Hello, this is Pizza Hut at Plaza Paseo, how may I help you?"

"Yes, are you guys delivering to Masaya right now?"

"No sir, unfortunately we are not able to deliver to Masaya currently due to everything that is happening. You can order for pick up, though."

"No, that's okay, I completely understand. Have a good night," I say before hanging up the phone.

I was not surprised, and I looked up the phone number for Papa Johns, the only other pizza delivery option in Masaya, and I called them.

"Hello, this is Papa John's in Masaya."

"Hi there. Are you currently able to deliver within Masaya?"

"Yes, we are delivering everywhere in Masaya. What would you like to order?"

"I'll have two family sized pizzas, one vegetarian and one with ham and cheese."

"Great, it should be delivered within 45 minutes," he told me. "Thank you very much."

Papa John's already knew where I lived and had my phone number on file, which was impressive because I had only ordered from them once before. Sometimes I forget about the prevalence of such advanced technology when living in Nicaragua because it is only available to a small percentage of the population. In the capital, where most of the country's wealth is located, it wouldn't be unusual for a business to use computers and electronic payment systems, but outside of the capital few businesses are able to afford such costly investments.

Satisfied that I would at least have pizza while under lockdown for the night, I laid down and looked at my phone. I had just gotten a text message from my current love interest Ricardo, a handsome Nicaraguan lawyer and college professor who lives in León.

"*Hola amor*," he wrote "Do you have time to video chat right now?"

Instead of texting back I just initiated the video chat, which he quickly accepted.

"*Hola Evan*," he said. "How are things in Masaya?"

"Things are definitely dicey here," I replied. "Police are liberally using tear gas and rubber bullets against civilians who have nothing but rocks to defend themselves. How are things in León?"

"Things are very similar here, *amor*," Ricardo sighed. "I am afraid to go outside of my house, but at the same time I want to join the protesters in the streets who are fighting for the rights of retirees."

"I understand, Ricardo, but I want for you to be safe," I admonished. "Please stay inside tonight."

In the background of our conversation, I heard the explosions getting louder and more frequent, as if the entire house were surrounded by the riots.

"Hold on Ricardo," I said, quickly standing up from my bed. "I need to check on something."

I walked over to open my bedroom door and investigate what was happening in the streets. As soon as I opened the door, I saw my mom, Loyda and Olinto with their backs against the wall at the front of our house. They all looked alarmed and I could see the clouds of gas and dark figures fighting through the lone window at the front of the house.

Without saying a word, Olinto puts a finger over his mouth and waves his other hand, signaling me to shut up and get back in my room.

Frightened, I walked back to my bed and picked up my phone.

"What is going on, Evan?" Ricardo asks me, visibly concerned on the tiny screen in my hand.

"The rioting is all around my house," I began.

Before I could finish the sentence, I hear my host family outside of my door screaming, "EVAN, get out here now!"

"I have to go Ricardo, I will talk to you later," I say while hanging up and jumping out of bed. I opened my bedroom door, and Loyda immediately covers my face with a cloth and rushes me to the back of the house, where she the whole family has gathered in the only bedroom fully insulated from the outdoors.

I didn't know what was happening at first, but I could see that our house was full of a white cloudy gas.

In the few seconds from when I had left my bedroom and entered the back room, my eyes started burning, despite the cloth. It felt as if a hundred hostile scorpions were forcing their way behind my eyes and into my head.

When I entered the back room, I saw my host mom and my young niece Stephanie washing their faces with bowls of water, and within a few seconds, my host siblings came in carrying our skinny dog.

It was clear to me now what had happened. Protesters all around my house had just been attacked by the police with tear gas, which has a tendency to spread out over large distances and fill empty spaces. My home, like most Nicaraguan homes, was built with large gaps between the walls and ceiling to allow fresh air and a breeze to pass through the house. When the tear gas canisters were deployed all around our house, the gasses seeped in from all sides and filled most of the rooms in our house.

Other than making sure that I was okay, everyone was silent and afraid. My host mom passed me a bowl of water and gestured for me to wash my eyes and face. I splashed the water on my face, giving special attention to my throbbing eyes, as well as my burning lips and nostrils. I tasted a hint of vinegar, which I had heard was essential to remove the chemicals in tear gas. Although the stinging pain in my eyes persisted, I tried to ignore it.

I looked at my phone and saw several worried text messages from Ricardo, who had no idea why I had suddenly hung up. Looking through his messages, I felt my eyes start to sting again—this time not from the tear gas. I could feel a lump form in my throat but one glance back at my host family forced me to choke it down. I knew that if I started to cry, they would all try to comfort me, but right now I just wanted to sit quietly and not have to explain my feelings.

Instead, I simply texted him, "My house was filled with tear gas, so my family and I are all tucked away in the back room, farthest away from the street."

Loyda finally breaks the silence. Looking at me, she says, "There is a warrant out for my arrest. Earlier today I was interviewed by a news channel about the protests, and I was very critical of the government."

"But is that all?" I asked. "They can't arrest you for speaking your mind on television."

"Well, they want to arrest me because of the interview that I gave, but to do so they fabricated other charges against me," she explained patiently. "They said that I assaulted a police officer during the protests."

"Did you assault a police officer?" I asked.

Loyda laughed, "Well not today, I didn't."

Considering Loyda's long and passionate political career, it wouldn't surprise me if she had thrown a few punches along the way.

"Don't worry, Evan," she said consolingly. "They have put out warrants for the arrest of hundreds of people, and they won't be able to capture all of us."

"What are you going to do?" I asked.

"Tonight, I will sneak out to a friend's house, and stay there," she replied. "After that, I will head to the mountains in the far north."

Before I had a chance to respond, my phone started ringing. Expecting it to be Ricardo, I grabbed my phone and answered immediately.

"Hello?"

"Yes, this is Papa John's," the voice on the other end said. "Here's the thing," he hesitated "We are not able to deliver your pizzas right now because your street is full of rioting."

Not knowing what else to do, I laughed.

The delivery man continued, "Is there another address that we could deliver these pizzas to? Perhaps a friend's house?"

"No," I replied. "I live here in this house and I am afraid that my friends don't want to pay for the pizzas."

"Well, can we try again to deliver them in a few hours?" he suggested. "They might get cold though."

"That is fine, these are hardly normal circumstances," I replied, trying not to laugh again at the outlandishness of the situation. "If you cannot deliver the order, I will understand completely."

I hung up the phone, shaking my head. I hadn't thought about the pizzas since I had ordered them. *What were they thinking?* I wondered bemusedly. *Why are they even still working?*

As I turned my attention back to my host family, my host mom looked at me and said, "Evan, have you contacted the Peace Corps yet? You might have to leave Masaya for a few days."

"I will give them a call," I replied. It was a good idea to get in touch with the Peace Corps' security team. "I think I should start packing a bag because I don't think I will be allowed to stay here while the riots are going on."

Once the tear gases had dispersed and the burning sensation in my eyes started to fade, I left our nook in the back of the house and returned to my bedroom. As soon as I shut the door I started to sob.

I didn't ever think this could happen. Nicaragua has always been so peaceful during my time here! Although I had suspected that the country would need to overhaul their political system sometime in the next decade, I never thought it would be so sudden or so violent.

I laid back down on my bed and hugged my pillow close to my body so that I had something to hold. A thousand questions were running through my mind—*Would I need to leave Nicaragua? Would the country devolve further into war? Would the military break down the door to my house tonight to arrest Loyda? If they do, what would they do to the rest of us?*

I wiped away my tears, and got out of bed. I pulled out my phone and called Marcelo Bancroft, the Safety and Security Director of Peace Corps Nicaragua.

Bancroft answered and listened intently as I described the shooting that I had witnessed, the tear gas that had filled my house, and the warrant out for Loyda's arrest.

"What do you want me to do?" I asked him.

He seemed tense and conflicted. Breaking the silence, he said "Fuck... I want you to stay inside your house tonight. I have a meeting at the embassy tomorrow morning at ten, and we will be discussing what to do then." He paused before continuing, "I would like to ask that you not tell any other volunteers about what you have seen so far. I don't want to worry them unnecessarily."

"I understand, I will keep it to myself," I replied slowly as thoughts began rapidly filling my head, faster than I could keep up with them. "But I don't know if I can wait until 10 am for an answer. The next round of protests is scheduled for tomorrow morning at nine. By the time you get the answer to me it may be unsafe to get out of Masaya."

He took a deep breath and considered that for a moment. "The truth is that you have a better idea of what is actually happening in Masaya than we do," he conceded. "If you feel the need to evacuate early tomorrow morning before the protests restart, then do it. Please."

Never having experienced something like this before, I wasn't sure what to do. I didn't feel completely unsafe in my house, but I knew that the neighboring city of Granada was experiencing much less rioting than Masaya.

Without really thinking, I reached for a bottle of sauvignon blanc that I had been saving and I started to drink. There is no way that I would have been able to sleep that night without a few glasses of wine.

At this point in the evening I was already dressed in my pajamas, but I knew that I would need to change. Thoughts were flooding my head so quickly, I couldn't tell which ones were rational or not.

At any time throughout the night, the police could break down our door to arrest Loyda, right? I wondered as my thoughts continued to spiral out of control. *If that were to happen, I would need to be wearing proper clothing and running shoes. Will I really need to run?* I thought nervously.

I erratically started to pack a small backpack. *What are you supposed to bring when you flee your home?* I thought while grabbing random pieces of clothing off my floor and throwing them into my bag. *My passport and cash. Those were obvious choices. Maybe nothing heavy,* I thought, looking at the small pile of books and work materials scattered on my desk. *I may have to run to avoid tear gas and bullets.*

I grabbed two bottles of water, some granola bars and tortillas, a scarf to protect myself from more tear gas, a spare tee shirt and my toothbrush. *I am packing for a two or three day evacuation to Granada, just until everything calms down, right?*

As I packed these basics, I began to cry again. This was not the Nicaragua I had known so well. Nicaraguans are friendly, and the government had always seemed well-intentioned, even if it was bureaucratic and inefficient.

What if I have to leave the country? I thought suddenly. The idea brought me to a full stop. Instead of rushing around my room, I stood frozen with pair of socks dangling from right hand, staring straight ahead like a deer in headlights. *Leave Nicaragua? It won't come to that... will it?*

As if in response to these intrusive thoughts, my phone buzzed, indicating a new text message from Jennifer, a colleague of mine from the Nicaraguan Ministry of Education.

It read, "Evan, I am so sorry that I won't be able to say goodbye to you."

When I saw the message, my stomach felt like it had shriveled up, and I started to cry harder. I put down my backpack, laid down and grabbed a pillow to sob into it yet again.

I knew that Jennifer didn't have any more information than I did, but she was more familiar with Nicaragua than I was. If she thought that I would be removed from the country, it must mean that these events were especially disturbing and out of the ordinary.

After a few minutes, the tears had stopped, but I continued to lay there. My whole body felt tense and numb as I considered what to do next.

Suddenly I heard the loud *BANG BANG BANG* of a fist, hammering the metal door at the front of our house.

This is it, I thought. *The police are here to arrest Loyda, and who knows what they will do to the rest of us.*

There was no sense in hiding, our home was tiny and there was nowhere that I could go. I began to feel the fear building up inside my chest.

Again the figure hit the door, *BANG BANG BANG*. He shouted a few words, but I couldn't make them out. My heart was beating so fast, I could hear it. The veins on my neck were felt like they going to pop out.

A few seconds go by, and the person repeats his words.

"Papa Juan's!" the figure yelled.

The pizzas! I exclaimed internally. *I had completely forgotten about the pizzas!*

At that point, it had been almost three hours since I had called in the order. With all of the anxiety and fear weighing me down, food was the last thing on my mind.

I grabbed my money and ran to the front door. When I opened the metal gate, I saw the tall delivery man with a cloth covering his face to avoid the tear gas throughout the city.

"Thank you very much," I said, taking the two pizzas and giving him a generous tip for his efforts. He grunted his approval and took off quickly down the now empty street.

After shutting and carefully locking and barring the door, I went to the living room and called out to my family to come get pizza.

I considered telling them about my initial reaction when I heard the banging on the door, but I decided that it would be better to keep it to myself.

"So will you be leaving tomorrow morning?" Loyda asked me as she grabbed her first slice.

"I think so," I replied solemnly "I don't want to stay here for another round of rioting tomorrow."

"You should leave here tomorrow at six or seven in the morning," she advised. "If you leave any later than that, you will risk encountering more riots."

"I will do that," I said, nodding my head at her advice. "Do you think there will be taxis?"

"Taxi drivers have to eat, too," she laughed. "They will be working as long as they can."

"Good to know," I smiled in reply. "I should get some sleep before tomorrow. Good night, Loyda."

After shutting the door to my room, I poured my third glass of wine and removed the backpack from my bed.

I knew from a few group chats that Crystal and I were the only Peace Corps Volunteers currently in Masaya, and that she wanted to leave the city as soon as possible. Before going to sleep, I coordinated with her to escape the city together the following morning.

I put on another podcast to drown out the sound of gunfire and explosions. That night I slept fully dressed and with my running shoes on—just in case.

The next morning, I woke up at six. Crystal and I had planned to meet at the north side of town on the highway in order to grab a bus or taxi out of Masaya.

Emerging from my bedroom, I looked around the house and was relieved to see everyone acting normal.

I found my host brother at the front of the house and asked, "Olinto, how is everything this morning?"

"Things are pretty normal at the moment, but everyone is getting ready for the next round of protests," he told me "Last night a group of soldiers came from Managua to enforce a curfew, but there wasn't too much violence. A group of people burned the Salesiano High School, but nobody is sure who's to blame. Others attempted to burn City Hall, but they were unsuccessful."

"Does it seem safe to go outside?" I asked.

"Right now, it is totally fine," Olinto said, gesturing to the open door.

The street was a bit emptier than it would have been on a normal day, but seemed otherwise normal. All of the bullets and tear gas canisters were gone, and people were walking around and riding bicycles, almost as if nothing had happened.

Could this have all been a nightmare? I wondered. *Why does everything seem so normal?*

I felt relieved that I wouldn't have to use my running shoes to dodge bullets during my evacuation, but I still felt unsettled.

My host mom emerged from the kitchen and turned to me. "You should head to Granada soon, while it is still calm."

"I know, *mamá*," I said "I packed my backpack last night and I will be meeting Crystal soon on the highway."

"When do you expect to return?" she asked.

"I would guess within 3 or 4 days, if everything calms down," I responded hopefully "the Peace Corps will want to make sure that there are no more protests here before they give me clearance to come back."

My mom looked unsatisfied with that answer.

"There is no way to know for sure when I will be back, or if the Peace Corps will make me leave the country for a while," I explained. "It all depends on what Ortega decides to do over the next few days. If he keeps violently repressing protests, I think that this could escalate even further. I hope it calms down soon though."

Olinto and my host mom nodded, indicating that this answer seemed more realistic.

"Well my son, you always have a home here in Masaya," she said. "We hope to see you again in a few days."

"Thank you, mom," I said as I hugged her goodbye. "By the way, where is Loyda?"

"She left very early in the morning, before the sun came up," she replied. "She has already gone into hiding, and even we aren't sure where she is. That is for the best." My host mother sighed, looking more tired than I've seen her in a long time. "Anyway, are you all ready to go to Granada?"

"Yes, I think I've got everything," I said. "I need to leave now to meet up with Crystal. I hope to see you guys in a few days, but until then, stay safe."

"Likewise, my son," my host mom said while giving me a last, strong embrace and kiss on the cheek.

Olinto gave me a hug and handed me my backpack from its spot on the floor. "Stay safe, *hermano*."

"You too," I said sadly.

They both walked with me to the front door and watched as I left our house and headed down the street.

I will be back in a few days, I thought. *Once the social security reforms are repealed, people will calm down and everything will go back to normal.*

Despite these optimistic thoughts, I couldn't ignore the bitter uncertainty in my stomach.

Once I arrived to the main street, I saw dozens of street cleaners hard at work sweeping up with their brooms and wooden carts. The sides of the carts were decorated with the traditional colors and slogans of the Sandinista government, and the uniforms of the cleaners were embroidered with the party's logo. Although I had seen this propaganda a thousand times, it had never seemed as sinister as it did that morning.

Does the government think that if it cleans up the evidence of their violent repression that people will forget it happened? The thought seemed crazy, but then again, nothing the government was doing seemed particularly rational.

I spotted a taxi heading north, which I flagged down. As I entered the small, dented vehicle, I felt relieved. *I am safe, and I will be back in just a few days,* I kept repeating to myself.

Since that day though, I have learned the fragile nature of life, which changes course without my permission. It has been half a year since I left Masaya and I have not yet been able to return.

The Nicaraguan government has become even more violent in their treatment of protesters, and has continued brutalizing and killing civilians by the hundreds.

Human rights organizations count between 300 and 500 dead, including many children and infants. One innocent killed by the police in Masaya was my 17 year old student, who was shot in the back by police while walking down the main street where I used to buy my vegetables. He wanted to go to college to become a veterinarian. His death nearly broke me.

Several of my other close Nicaraguan friends have become refugees, fleeing to Panama, Costa Rica and Honduras for their own safety.

The Nicaraguan government has decided to give ski masks to police and members of their paramilitary forces to hide their identities during the massacres. Government contracted snipers have been placed in most urban centers, such as Masaya, León and Managua, where they have killed dozens of civilians for the crime of walking in public.

After being evacuated to the US, I have kept in close contact with my Nicaraguan friends, but I am often left without words for their pain and constant struggles.

Ricardo and I no longer talk. He has slipped into a deep depression, and when I told him that the Peace Corps would not be sending me back to Nicaragua, he felt betrayed—although I'm still not sure if he blames me or his government.

Seeing the country that I love descend into a chaotic and bloody landscape has worn me down and taxed me in more ways than I can describe.

I didn't ever think this would happen.

EVERYONE'S ASLEEP
H. HOFFMAN
GRANADA

It's three in the morning when I get back home, and everyone is asleep. I approach the house stealthily, in the silence of the night—darker and more ominous than ever. Cautious of the perverse eyes and ears of government informants who are always lurking, scattered on every street corner, hidden, almost unknown. Nowadays it is impossible to know whom to trust.

A comrade accompanies me on part of the walk, while others watch us from afar.

"I am tired," he whispers in an attempt to maintain the silence of the night. "We have been at this for days, but I will not rest, not until Ortega is gone."

I listen and gesture for him to be quiet as we stop at the corner, where only two days prior a Sandinista official was recruiting kids to help attack the peaceful protesters—to attack *us* with mortars, knives, machetes and homemade weapons all for the price of 200 *córdobas*[10] and a plate of food. These kids form the famous *Juventud Sandinista*, or Sandinista Youth. Their most recent attack against us lasted more than an hour, but the supporters of our resistance group from the northern and western neighborhoods of Granada came to our aid, and we were able to withstand most of the onslaught. We forced the mercenaries and the supporters of the Ortega regime to retreat, while others in our group stayed to defend our *tranque*[11]. Those of us who stayed at the *tranque* defended its three lateral entrances, protecting ourselves with tin shields, and firing mortars. During the battle, one of us was shot in the head, immediately collapsing. The bullet grazed his head but luckily did not penetrate the skull. Bleeding heavily, the duty medic at our *tranque* ran to treat him in the midst of the battle. After a long fight, Ortega's henchmen finally fled, beaten and wounded. It was a great victory that we could not have fathomed a month ago—that day gave us hope. I poked my head around the corner; ahead of us was an empty street blanketed by a gloomy sky.

---

[10] At the time of publication, 200 córdobas was worth approximately 6.25 US dollars.

[11] Tranque: An improvised barricade and roadblock, typically made from cobblestones and sandbags. Their primary purposes are to protect inhabitants from paramilitary and police brutality, and to disrupt commerce and the flow of traffic. Historically, this tactic has been employed by Nicaraguans resisting repressive government forces.

"Tonight has been very calm," I say to my companion. It was as calm as it could be given the circumstances. Various alerts had put us on guard, ready to defend ourselves, but tonight we didn't have to. Every night they stalk us, watching us from their motorcycles, 100 meters from the perimeter of our *tranque*. Some of them shine lights on us, while others hide in the darkness watching our every move. This continues until one of us discovers their hiding place and outs their position on social media, using the hashtag of our movement. Social media has been a great ally in our fight.

"Yes, hopefully our victory the other day taught them a lesson," he replied. "They'll learn that you can't buy loyalty. A couple bucks are nothing compared to our patriotic cause."

"From here on, I will go solo, just keep an eye out for me," I told him. "That house over there is full of rats and it's best that I proceed alone, to make less noise. If they spot me, they will know where I live and I don't want to put my family in jeopardy." In a few of the houses, people were still awake; one of my neighbors works nights. I pass by the house of a policeman who lives on my block, but surely he's asleep by now. The previous weekend, I had seen strange people in his house. He and I know each other well, so I asked him who they were.

"They are dressed as civilians, but in reality they're here to gather information for the government," he told me. "They left their truck out front, and they are wandering the city to take photos of anyone suspected of aiding the resistance. They have followed kids from the cemeteries and the *tranques*, and now the government knows where they live. Don't be surprised when the kids go missing. It seems like something out of a movie, I struggle to believe it myself, but after all that we have seen so far, we shouldn't underestimate them."

When I finally arrive at my house, I look all around me before going inside, to see if anyone had been watching me. I no longer had a cloth covering my face, I had pulled it off two blocks ago. I walk onto the front porch and I stay there, sitting on the ground, dejected. I don't want to go home now,. I only want to go home once all of this is over so I can tell my mom that "Finally, Ortega is gone." Unfortunately, that is still a long ways away. Nostalgia invaded my chest in that moment, in the same way that it used to be filled with hope, platonic love or an anxious idea that was worthy of a poem, a letter or a daydream.

Listless, together with the apparent calmness of the night, images of the past few days came to my mind. All I can do is try to stop the tears from falling. I won't be able to sleep, and soon I will have to go to work. Another day dead-tired at my job is nothing compared to the sacrifice that more than eighty families have made so far. Tonight I will only write a little.

> *Everyone's asleep, everyone's asleep*
> *while an inconsolable mother cries*
> *for her murdered son and others fear*
> *that the same fate will soon befall their children.*

A student implores God
to wake up tomorrow with his life,
because today he carried out the act of suicide
that is revealing himself to be against the government,
anxiety and fear devour him, the trench in which he lies is hell.

The country is a fire that does not ignite or that has already died out,
in its embers it dies painfully,
spreading out murder, terror and fear.
False hope gives us an expert lash.
We are in his territory, in his zone,
all of his cunning is coming afloat,
he is the devil disguised as a man.

Everyone's asleep, everyone's asleep
while a woman who was a wife,
now is alone, unconsciously swaying back and forth in pain.
She has lost her support, she has lost her rock.
She finishes her prayer with an "amen,"
her future is now a mystery.

Chaos, chaos in my country, and death.
Where youth is an impending crime;
mortars and slingshots are up against AK 47s
and warm blood spills out,
another Nica, today has met his fate.

Masaya raises its banner;
Monimbó is in the fight,
weapons fighting against art,
all throughout the city it is heard
"Liberty, liberty and justice"

Artisans fall for the greed of one man,
and my country is torn in two.

A child on the ground begs for his life,
with a police boot on his neck,
followed by a roar and a flash,
a shot executed in the chest,
another martyr of the new dawn.
The street will be his final bed.

Greetings to the valiant pastors
who in an act of whole daring
are in the streets, branded with rebellion
mediating between the just and the oppressors,
between bullets, rocks and mortars
they go between the temples and the barracks
asking for the liberation of the prisoners
and for piety, an end to the cruel acts.
They have heard the clamor of the people,
mercenaries come with their hoods
and the priests are in this fight,
marching with Christ to the frontline.

Everyone's asleep, everyone's asleep
while I send God my prayer
for those who suffer, cry and fear.
Nicaragua will once again be a Republic.

As the crisis progressed, Granada was separated into various factions. I, of course, am part of the resistance, which fights for change using peaceful protests. There are also the Orteguistas, who support the genocidal president and live in secrecy, compiling information. We all knew about them, but did not expect them to be capable of these atrocities. There are also the hired mercenaries, chiefly made up of delinquents from the western neighborhoods of Granada. Next, there are those who are neutral and try to convince themselves that everything is normal. They go to work, go out with their friends, and have fun like nothing has happened. The final group, in my opinion, are the merchants, who after the sacking of the city in the final days of April, have unified and declared that nobody should enter the commercial areas after nightfall. They lock down the area with barricades, allowing no one to enter.

The Orteguista mercenaries are unable to stay still and probably have orders to create chaos. They roam the city center, committing crimes. This forced the surrounding neighborhoods to construct barricades to keep them out, particularly to block the vehicles that come at night to fire machine guns at houses, inciting anarchy. During the days everything seems normal. The area with the most tension is the *tranque*, where both vehicles and people are brought together. But at nightfall, the city is a lawless no man's land. The police have orders to allow all acts of violence to cause fear and anxiety. The central and eastern neighborhoods have started to clash at night. "They are gang fights," say the Sandinistas. Those of us who are better informed know that the clashes have been politically motivated.

The day after my sleepless night writing poetry, the *tranque* was more relaxed. It was not as tiring as when I had to be in charge of something, such as defending one of the walls or directing traffic through the *tranque*. It is not easy arguing with everyone who wants to pass through the roadblocks: the truckers, the merchants, people going to their jobs or their homes, and even more so dealing with the other members of our resistance movement, each of them wishing to impose their own idea of how to do things, without organization or chains of command. This movement is just starting out, and each head is home to its own world. Although I have come to realize that patriotism and heroism have nothing to do with academic education, the lack of it makes matters complicated. There are some among us who wish to sow chaos and take advantage of the crisis to get a bit of money for food or to fuel their vices.

At every moment they challenge you, ask who put you in charge, or if you have enough people to properly defend the *tranque*. They start to charge drivers a fee to pass through, and they wish to keep it for themselves. At every moment, someone stands up and says "Let them through already," while someone goes to the line of trucks waiting to pass, asking them for money in exchange for expedited passage. Everybody wants to take over the management of the *tranque*; contending with these challenges is a regular occurrence. It has tested my patience and my integrity, but it has gone fairly well so far, never having resulted in violence. There are always others at the *tranque* who revive my faith in humanity; there are so many in need of money, with only hunger in their stomachs and nothing to lose, who rise to defend our cause.

Others at the *tranque* would tell me passionately, "We are not delinquents. We all want the same thing—for the murderer to be removed from power." Hearing this only gives me more strength and conviction. There are so many of us who yearn for a free Nicaragua, from the depths of our hearts.

During the daytime, people keep us company and the *tranque* is a happy place. You can hear the chants of freedom, the songs of the heroes and martyrs of April, the salutations to the students of the tranque and their bravery. People dance, the *tranque* is full, and *señoras* bring us food and drink. The marches and peaceful protests pass by and people take photos in the barricades wearing masks and holding mortar launchers. Some of them stay and join the fight, deciding to contribute to the cause with more than just a post or a status update on social media.

I have been very impressed by the conviction of some of these young boys and girls who have stayed here day and night. By now they know and respect each other. Respect is something which is earned, and these young people have earned it with sweat. By nightfall, we are fewer, but the most dedicated among us stay—those who have taken on this cause as their own, and are wholeheartedly willing to fight for freedom. Despite their fear, they continue onwards and speak of liberation, peace and justice for our fallen countrymen.

At night they form groups in the *tranque* to share their experiences; some faced the riot police in the early days of the revolution back in April. Some of them show off their injuries and bullet wounds from the battles before the local truce between the police and the citizens of Granada, which attempted to salvage the damaged economy. We stay energized by taking our fight seriously—maintaining it in our hearts until we attain our freedom. Many of us have children and say "I don't want my children to live through a war, my children are so young... but I don't want them to be killed by the government in a few years like they've killed so many of us already. I am going to fight to put an end to this." Their intense stories leave my skin bristling. Each hour there are fewer of us. Personally, I have been here for a few days. I came here to deliver medical supplies for the wounded, but then I started to help raise the barricades with cobblestones and sandbags. In the end, I decided to stay the night. That first night at the *tranque*, I saw the conviction of the others, motivating me to stay longer. They say that they're willing to give their lives for the freedom of our country—I never thought I would witness something like this.

It's important for you to understand the philosophy behind this form of peaceful protest. The *tranque* puts pressure on the economy of the country and suffocates the government both internally and externally, at least according to what I have been told. The neighboring countries begin to complain about the delay in commerce, and for that reason our principal objective is to hold up cargo trucks, sometimes delaying them as long as 24 hours at the *tranque*, although some of the young people here think that it should be longer. The genocidal president is also a great capitalist and his businesses are affected by the slow commerce caused by the *tranques* throughout the country. Soon the government will have to rely on their capital reserves, and eventually they will have to negotiate... or at least that is what we hope. Even with their socialist views and anticapitalistic sentiments, all Nicas know that the country is full of large businesses, the illicit ones being of particular importance. None of these companies are willing to lose their holdings. But I digress.

Women are also present in this fight. In the southern *tranque*, a veteran woman nicknamed *la morena* gives orientations and organizes new people who have joined the movement. She gives mortar launchers to some and shields to others, and she tells them what to do in the case of an attack. A few days ago, I saw her on the frontline. She was sleeping in some bushes when we were told that the attack was imminent. Without hesitation, she jumped up and ran to the northern *tranque*, carrying a mortar launcher and a backpack heavy with ammunition. As she ran there, she covered her face with cloth and yelled, "In positions, without fear!"

In the northern *tranque* there is another young woman, fair-skinned, slender and attractive. They call her *la flaca* and she lifts the cloth covering her face so that she can take drags from her cigarette. Usually she sits silently in the barricades, while the boys joke around, always attentive of what she can spot from her vantage point. She carries her mortar launcher as if it were an extension of her arm, and sometimes shoots straight up in the air, so the opposition knows we're always alert. Shooting one handedly, her arm covered in tattoos—she is the utter vision of a "vandal warrior," to use the term coined by the genocidal presidential couple, which we have started using ironically ever since. There are other women guarding the food, medical supplies, Molotov cocktails and everything else we have to defend ourselves.

One afternoon, they captured a young man who they claim is part of the Sandinista Youth. He came a few times a day to the *tranque* to record videos, which we found on his cell phone when he was captured. He says nothing, but there is fear in his eyes—probably a fear of what this insurrection entails. They are not afraid of being attacked by us; they benefit from the fact that our fight is peaceful. It doesn't matter to them if they are captured by us, because they know that even if they've hurt our cause, we will let them go. We talk to them and tell them to join the people, to open their eyes, but it is too much for them to take in. I never thought that such fanaticism could exist; they have been bought with meager amounts. Sometimes we feel so excluded in this world that merely belonging to an organization makes us feel valued and important—whether the organization is good or bad.

The days pass by and many of the youths already recognize me, surely by my physical features, as our faces are always covered. They wait for me so that I can tell them what I know and what I have seen today in Managua or Masaya. Sometimes they simply want to know what I have read on social media because not all of them have cell phones or the internet to stay informed.

"Don't let them get you," I always tell them. "If you see them getting close, run. Your lives are important." While I show my comrades photos and videos, I tell them about the different youths who have been captured in the *tranques* and barricades. They are tortured and their bodies are dumped in the streets or empty lots. In the best of cases, they torture you, asphyxiate you, they pull out your nails, and they traumatize you psychologically; because of this, the majority of those who are captured never return to the protests. Sometimes I think that I am wrong to show them such things—they may become afraid and desert the cause. However I firmly believe that we have the right to know what is happening, to be conscious of the situation, and that we should not be deceived. If we choose to continue fighting, we do so knowing the potential consequences.

We constantly receive threats. They tell us that the riot police are coming or that the Sandinista Youth are only four blocks away. To others, they send threats directly to their cell phones. We receive anonymous texts saying things like, "We already know where you live and what time you left your house. We are watching you. Your grandmother is alone. Your younger siblings are alone." These messages make us question our participation in the resistance. This tactic is cowardly. In reality we know what these delinquents are capable of. They go as low as you can imagine, they have no conscience. For them it is war. It pains me deeply that my country has fallen into the hands of delinquents and killers.

What kind of future can we hope for? Has an armed insurrection ever installed an honest and just government? I think not. How did we not realize this before? This time is different though, the peaceful protesters have the slogan,

Patria libre y vivir[12]. Nicaragua will once again be an illustrious and civilized nation; this is my conviction.

Each time I go to the *tranque*, everyone watches as I approach the barricades. They aim their mortar launchers at me. I am okay with this—we have to be wary of every person who approaches us. A few days ago, in the *tranques* of Masaya, a few police officers in civilian clothing got too close and were able to draw their weapons on the youths. They kidnapped a group of ten peaceful protesters and took them away. Now we must be more careful.

"Hairy armpit," I yell once I'm within earshot. This phrase is a password, invented by the protesters, which alludes to the unattractive physical features of Ortega's wife and vice president, Rosario Murillo.

"You go with the trumpet-lipped man," respond several of them in chorus, alluding to the president himself. "Let him through" they say, while others call out "He is part of the resistance." Each day we choose a new password to identify ourselves to each other.

"Have you seen Z1?" I ask to the air.

"He is in the southern *tranque*," says one of the young men.

---

[12] *Patria libre y vivir* translates as "Free homeland and life." This slogan is a distinct take on the national hero Sandino's term *"Patria libre o muerte,"* meaning "Free homeland or death," which was adopted by the Sandinistas during their struggle to oust the Somoza dynasty.

Z1 is the captain of my team and I am his shadow whenever I am there. I am always one step behind him, vigilant. We walk the perimeter with a few other young protesters, surveying the surrounding area. We walk all the way to the back of the stopped traffic, saying to each person "Good morning, good afternoon, or good evening *señor* or *señora*. We do not charge a fee at this *tranque*. Do not give money to anyone. We are looking for people who are in some sort of danger or who are sick, to allow them to pass through without waiting. Ambulances and fire trucks have priority."

In the early morning, after taking a break from walking around the *tranque*, which stretches two hundred meters from barricade to barricade, we share some ideas.

"Z1, it has been days since we have received any serious threats, this is strange," I say. "Something is awry, something is brewing."

"That much is obvious," he replies. "Each day that we go without an attack, we must be more alert. But it is true that Masaya and Carazo have formed a shield which prevents police and paramilitary forces from reaching Granada, however they are not the only forces that the government controls. They must be plotting something as we speak."

In fact, that was that case. From the looks of it, some paramilitaries were providing basic training to mercenaries and government fanatics to make an offensive. Upon receiving an arsenal of guns from Managua during the first few days of June, they attacked the city of Masaya. This attack was spine chilling and violent, with dozens of deaths and disappearances—nobody could contain it. The heroic people of Monimbó faced them for the longest. On that day, the battle lasted seven hours.

The *tranques* and other forms of peaceful pressure come and go. It is for that reason that I tell the young people in the *tranque* not to fight against a force that they cannot possibly defeat—it is better to flee than be captured and tortured. As long as we live, we can put pressure on the government, but if we lose our lives, there is no going back. The lives of those infamous government agents and their entourage are not more important than the lives of any protester. Their hands are stained with blood and they are "morally dilapidated," according to Victor Cuadras, a university student and leader. Cuadras helped form the Civil Alliance, which represents much of the Nicaraguan people in the negotiations with the government. These negotiations seek a solution—an end to the current social, economic and humanitarian catastrophe that our country is facing.

Although the details of the following story have not been confirmed by multiple parties, it was reported by a priest. On the night of June 4th, 2018, a police truck entered the zone between the central and eastern neighborhoods of Granada, opening fire on two positions of the resistance. This provocation sparked a bloody battle that lasted an entire day.

These police attacks were just the beginning. In the early morning of June 5th, the mercenaries and government fanatics joined the fight. The eastern neighborhoods of

Granada—the epicenter of infamous Sandinista Youth forces—had been waiting to invade the central neighborhoods for days, to defeat the resistance based there. That morning, they did just that.

The inhabitants of the city center repelled them with mortars, rocks and whatever they could find, but it was not enough. Some of their mortars contained as much as one pound of gunpowder, creating large explosions. The state-sponsored aggressors were loaded with firearms, and there was no way the resistance could hold them off. At around six in the morning, the police forces and Sandinista Youth were able to smash through one of the barricades protecting the city center, and tragedy ensued. Some members of the resistance were wounded by the bullets and collapsed. Chepe, an adolescent, was the first death in the city during this insurrection. There were photos and videos of the man who shot him: a merchant, a Sandinista, an Orteguista who stole a youth's life. A 38 caliber bullet struck his chest.

The inhabitants of the city center were under siege and cried out for help from whoever could reach them. Sandinistas were threatening to burn down their houses. Many were physically pulled from their homes and kidnapped, especially those who had supported and directed the opposition. The Orteguistas had lists of names and addresses from the government informants who had done their work in secrecy.

The response to their plea was immediate. The forces who guarded our *tranque* met and quickly agreed on the best course of action. Although a few would have preferred to continue guarding the *tranque,* the call to aid the central neighborhoods was enough for us to choose a priority.

"We will leave this for now, and we can reconstruct it later" they said, referring to the *tranque.* The resistance burst forth from the *tranque*: men, women, and youth. They came running, riding on motorcycles and bikes, or any way they could in order to liberate the city center. The fight was inflamed.

Around seven in the morning, the battle was in full force. The wounded were transported to hospitals by both sides, and minutes later, more men in ski masks with firearms arrived—paramilitaries in Granada. *Where did they come from? Paramilitaries in Granada!* We couldn't believe it.

We had to pull back, to save our own lives. We ceded no land, but were unable to advance. The call for aid was interdepartmental; the resistance asked for help from the movements in the other municipalities of Granada, and from nearby cities. Within half an hour, dozens of our supporters had entered the city on foot through the cemetery, but the arrival of a bus load of reinforcements was the most important addition to our fight. Diriomo, Diriá, Nandaime, Catarina and the Pueblos Blancos formed one group of reinforcements who came to our aid, giving us a renewed energy and hope. Then the ferocious Monimboseños, coming all the way from Masaya, arrived in Granada to reinforce us. They were few in number, but with their valor and boldness, they spearheaded the liberation of the city center.

By mid-morning the government mobs had all but retreated from the central park, and the fight moved to the main street of the city. The Monimboseños carved their way through the middle of the street, advancing and launching mortars and rocks along the way. There was no holding them back. Each time a step further. "Not one step back, we go forward!" they yelled. They were a shining example of bravery and fury. This sentiment was contagious and spread throughout the whole resistance. The wounded were attended to by medics that had devoted their service to the movement. The most severely injured were taken to the hospital, but some of the wounded stood up and continued fighting. It was incredible to see such conviction and adrenaline-fueled fervor. The mobsters became cowards; the more they retreated, the more fear overcame them. It seems to me that the Orteguistas were not able to defeat a force of equitable size, in spite of their superior weaponry. The mercenaries always have to use something to get the upper hand. They are unable to extinguish the roar of the people.

This was the turning point in the battle, in which the false ideals and selfish convictions of the mercenaries melted away. They only care about their paychecks, which of course will run out one day just like their thirst for blood. Scared, they went off in search of what had been promised to them. According to their own testimony, the pay which was promised to them by the government was never delivered, and as a result, the nearly defeated and inflamed mob of mercenaries irately broke into the City Hall of Granada in search of their pay, or something of value to replace it. The paramilitaries could not keep control of their own hired mobs and the police in civilian clothing fled in fear. At that moment, full chaos erupted from afternoon and lasted into the night. This confrontation had resulted in one of the most tragic losses of life in Granada, since the invasion of US pirates in the nineteenth century.

Opportunists from the most dangerous parts of the city joined the illicit festivities that followed. The government's refusal to pay the mercenaries lead to the City Hall of Granada and the House of the Sandinista Party being targeted. As revenge, the mercenaries razed both buildings in flames, then continued on to any business that represented a chance at scoring some loot.

The resistance dispersed, and returned to their various municipalities and homes to stave off looting. This was no longer a sociopolitical matter. By nightfall, you could see people strutting with their newly stolen goods. All of the businesses along the commercial street were sacked, and some were burnt. This was a day of terror.

This time the barricades were not being raised in the eastern and central ends of town; it was not them who needed to gather their forces and build a wall to protect themselves. Instead it was the police. At the police station, officials had left their barracks to pull the cobblestones from a nearby street, and build a protective barricade around themselves. They feared for their lives; they feared that after burning the City Hall and the House of the Sandinista Party that the mercenaries would go looking for those who recruited them, incited them and hired them in the first place. The police were hiding in their barracks and all of the streets leading to the police station were blocked with cobblestone barricades. The day of chaos, fire and death turned to night.

Following the battle in Granada, I returned to my home, where I now sit. My house is closed and locked up, with all of the bolts in place. Every type of sound could be heard from afar, in the silence of the night. There was laughter, cackles, screams, explosions. The night will be long and tragic.

We have to be informed, in communication with our neighbors and friends. On social media, I've heard that the members of my movement have gone to the streets to help recoup whatever they can after the sacking. Today there are no *tranques* in Granada; the Orteguistas took advantage of the battle to tear them down.

Once I start to reflect, when the adrenaline stops running through my body, the images resurface in my mind— everything that is happening, everything that has already occurred. It is not a movie; it is not a dream. The dead will never come back to life. Those who have disappeared have not come back.

There are innumerable images on social media of pain and despair. Of mothers sobbing for their children who haven't come home to ask for a plate of food. Of mothers who will never again hear the laughter and complaints of their children. Of mothers who cry inconsolably. The mothers are the epicenter of the uprising; their hearts are incomplete. Their hearts are broken. The pain is reflected in their eyes. It is impossible for me to keep from crying. Tonight, I don't think I will be able to sleep. Although weariness persuades me to close my eyes, empathy keeps me awake. This nightmare is one that the entire country wishes to wake from soon.

Now... I am only going to write a little.

AND THE STARS WERE SHINING
ROBERTO CARLOS PÉREZ
MANAGUA

In the memory of Lizandro Chávez Alfaro

E lucevan le stelle…
ed olezzava la terra
stridea l'uscio dell'orto…
e un passo sfiorava la rena…
Entrava ella fragrante,
mi cadea fra le braccia.
Giacomo Puccini, Tosca

Tonight I am the Duke of Mantua. The hall is overflowing. Soon I will be on stage dressed in a doublet embroidered with gold threads and a red beretta. And although the only newspaper which we have not yet acquired says that the only people who come to see me are employed by my father, deep down I know that everyone acclaims me. They throw me yellow roses, like Enrico Caruso, because they know that they are my favorite.

I have carefully warmed up my voice to be heard throughout the theater, so that they don't say that I cannot sing, as a critic opined when I played the role of the tormented painter Cavaradossi, in Tosca. That critic has already been taken care of, and I doubt that he will come to say anything tonight.

The breeze from Lake Managua reaches the theater. The people begin to take their seats to see the opera *Rigoletto*, of which I am also the producer. Because in this country one must do everything—I have decided to be their guide to culture. That's why I have brought eighty Italian singers to Nicaragua.

Lying are those who say that I am pilfering the State's money to satiate my wish to be an opera singer. Government employees have bought enough tickets to cover the costs of production and I am sure that none of them protested.

Mom is in the front row, greeting dignitaries and journalists. Dad is seated by her side. He has been taciturn for some time. He barely discusses with her how to manage the fate of our country. She is the one who governs. Thanks to her diligence, both clergymen and laypeople have come to see me. This is because she says that our government must be Christian, socialist, and of solidarity.

Today she is back to her usual ways. She decided to wear a striped dress, one of the most horrendous, and those bracelets and rings that everyone laughs at. But nobody dares to say anything because the Sandinista Youth is there to defend her.

Dad is also shameless. Nothing is further from his thoughts than putting on a tuxedo. How I wish he would at least wear a collared shirt. His mustache is old-fashioned and the thick glasses he refuses to take off exacerbate his age.

From the dressing room, I see the Trees of Life. Why did it occur to mom to plant those pieces of rubbish along the boardwalk and throughout the rest of the city? She is so eccentric—she has neither the good taste for decorating the city nor for dressing herself, but it is best not to tell her such things. She is capable of taking away my businesses, or the possibility of performing at La Scala, or even becoming president.

My hands are already sweating. In the rehearsals, the director—a chubby blond who was educated in Florence and who claims to be an expert in Verdi's operas— stopped the orchestra several times to point out that my chest voice was not giving the final *la* of *La donna e mobile*.
I wanted to raise my voice and respond that he is just another employee, and I am the boss. And when he told me that my Italian pronunciation is terrible and that I did not mark contrast between one sentence and another in the famous aria, he suggested that I listen to Pavarotti. How mistaken he is! I learned Italian with the best teachers

and I have already listened to Pavarotti. I know he would have applauded me.

I don't know why I sweat so much. It's just that I am distracted by the problems of the interoceanic canal that my father wants to build. They distract me from the *recitatives,* the transitions that separate the arias or something like that, as the fat Italian explained to me in his horrible Spanish.

Those *recitatives* are important in this opera. But the peasants' complaints kept me from sleeping well last night. It worries me that every day they protest more. They say that we stole their lands, and they've also started to say that we are killing them. Sleep is very important for a tenor of my stature. I don't know why I involved myself in the canal. Oh well... mom promised me that she would take charge of the matter.

I only want the best for this country. The canal will bring jobs, and moreover we will have the money from the businessman in Beijing. What difference does it make if the canal is Chinese? In this country, as my dad says, we must mobilize the economy; although many say that what we are doing is merely a front for us to appropriate indigenous lands.

We have built aquatic parks, a boardwalk on the shores of the lake, and a baseball stadium. And if that weren't enough, we decorated the city, because although my mother's trees are horrendous, when seen from afar with all of their lights, they are another thing entirely. It is like being in Paris during Christmas, and here in Managua, it is Christmas all year. It is like being drugged. My friends say that it is a cerebral stimulation. Maybe it is holy.

Who can say that a city like the one we are building does not have a grand economy? Ingrates. If those poor people were allowed to make decisions, they would be in the hands of the United States, or even worse, in their own hands. For that reason, my father says we must strengthen ties with Russia. And with Cuba. Venezuela is no longer of use to us.

Now things are getting better with the calls from the Russian president; and they will be even better if we can negotiate a military base in Nicaragua. Then we would really be swimming in money! Imagine what it would be like to have the Russians here! As a sign of goodwill, we've bought fifty war tanks from them. The only complication, as always, is the United States.

But in this moment, none of that matters. I must only think of tonight. I could have been Rigoletto; however, I was not born to be a hunchback, and even less so a jester. I was raised to lead and be president. And also to have many women. For that reason, I performed so well in *Questa o quella*, the aria in which the Duke speaks of his innumerable conquests; although, the fat man did not like my performance. I don't know what he wants. I've decided to replace him.

Gilda, the daughter of Rigoletto, must die. Tonight she will be played by a lovely and delicate singer who makes the theater vibrate, and that worries me. The Duke of Mantua cannot be eclipsed. What would my friends and all of the country say, upon seeing me become a runner-up?

I have ordered one of my television stations to broadcast the opera live, so that it is clear that my labor is simply to disseminate the arts and be remembered in history as the first son of two Nicaraguan presidents to have performed at La Scala.

The lights have been turned off. There is absolute silence. I look in the mirror and I see the country devoted at my feet. What I do, I do in spite of many who say that I am the spoiled son of my parents.

I close my eyes, breathe slowly and walk towards the stage. I feel the satisfied gaze of the public upon me. Like the Duke of Mantua, I will get what is mine, taking the applause and the yellow roses that I love so much.

This story was written by Roberto Carlos Pérez, envisioning the perspective of Laureano Ortega.

THE MOTHER'S DAY MASSACRE
RYAN W. N.
MANAGUA

Me duele respirar,
pero un día Nicaragua, una vez más será libre!
It hurts me to breath,
but one day Nicaragua, once more will be free!

This afternoon I witnessed firsthand a peaceful march, in protest of the brutal dictatorial regime of Daniel Ortega that has murdered over 80 people. In the march there were women, men and children of all ages exercising their right to protest. At about 5.15/30 pm as I was approaching the end point (about 500-700 meters away), the police, paramilitary and snipers started to attack members of the public. 4 people have been confirmed dead and more than 20 have been injured. The Nicaraguan government has no desire to uphold the human rights of its citizens. Unfortunately it is too far from home for many of you reading this from the USA and Europe, and so the media isn't doing a good job of reporting the situation. With over 80 killed already, on Mother's Day here in Nicaragua, there are many mothers who have lost their children and many more who don't know their children's whereabouts. Imagine losing your child or brother or sister! Wake up, world—a massacre is occurring! #FueraOrtegaMurillo #SOSNicaragua #MeDueleRespirar

The anger, anguish and helplessness I felt when I wrote the above post on my Facebook page on the night of May 30th 2018 still penetrates my soul to this day. The feeling of knowing too well the suffering of so many, in the place I came to call home, coupled with the inability to do anything that will shape the outcome of the political massacre that is manifesting in Nicaragua can, at times, be tremendously overwhelming.

My evolution into a Nicaraguan enthusiast, into someone who has become obsessed with this breathtakingly beautiful country, full of some of the warmest and friendliest people I have ever met, began back in May 2009. Two weeks after finishing the most important exams at my high school, I listened to a presentation from a London-based NGO talking about their expedition program to Costa Rica and Nicaragua. Not knowing much about either of these two distinct neighboring countries, that same night I went home and scoured the Internet for hours reading about Costa Rica and Nicaragua. The cost of the excursion was high, but I was determined that during the summer of 2010, I would travel to Central America and so I began fundraising enthusiastically and working a part time job in a supermarket. When summer 2010 came around, I was by no means disappointed.

It was a warm summer afternoon in the rural community where we—myself and 11 other volunteers—were working and living in northern Nicaragua, in the region of Estelí. A little over two weeks into my time in Central America and the start of my second week in Nicaragua, I listened attentively to the community leader as he talked about his experiences during the Nicaraguan Civil War of the 1980s. Don Hector was a stocky man, about 5 foot 7 with a protruding belly, a perfectly shaped thick and bushy moustache whose expression always seemed to be a little distant. I did my best to put my basic high school Spanish to use, and with the help of one of my team leaders who was bilingual, I held on to every word as Don Hector depicted his traumatic civil war experiences. He told me of how after the Sandinistas overthrew the Somoza dynasty dictatorship, Ronald Reagan funded those who opposed the Sandinistas, the *Contras,* and a 9 year civil war ensued. Reagan feared another successful communist/socialist Latin American state and despised Daniel Ortega, a Sandinista leader. For these reasons, Reagan vowed to combat the Sandinistas.

Haunted by his memories, Don Hector told me how he watched his best friend burn alive as a *Contra* bomb hit his squadron's station. He depicted the horror he felt when he shot and killed his first enemy combatant. As his story ended he lifted up his t-shirt to show me his shrapnel wounds and told me to look carefully at his left hand that was missing three fingertips—all wounds from the war.

Don Hector and others I met in this rural community spoke highly of the Sandinistas. There was a certain enthusiasm and hope amongst those I talked to. Daniel Ortega was serving the final year of his second presidential term, after a sixteen year gap in which others governed the nation. Some members of the community proudly showed me and the other volunteers the cows, geese and hens that Daniel had gifted them.

I later learned though my studies that Daniel Ortega was referred to as Daniel to make him appear approachable and to represent himself as an everyday Nicaraguan. Moreover, I learned that the animals given to many people from the countryside—*the campesinos*—were donated by the Chinese government through various aid programs. The Sandinista party skillfully divvied out these donations to win over the *campesinos* in anticipation of the municipal and presidential elections.

There was hope amongst most of the *campesinos* that Daniel would lift them out of poverty. As I spent the next two months in Costa Rica, I learned from some of my Nicaraguan friends that Daniel had pretty high approval ratings and that those who opposed him generally felt that despite his flaws, he was still the best of a bad bunch of leaders who had governed Nicaragua over the last 100 years. After all it was Daniel Ortega, I was told, who as part of the Sandinista National Liberation Front, freed Nicaragua from the brutal Somoza family that had governed with an iron hand.

Returning home to the UK after that summer, I continued researching Nicaragua. I changed my university degree from Law to Hispanic Studies and International Relations, and over the course of my five year degree that took me overseas to the US and South America, I wrote essays and gave presentations on numerous topics relating to Nicaraguan history, politics, society and art. I returned to Nicaragua in 2014 during my university summer vacation with the same London-based NGO, but this time my own opinion about the Ortega government was far less enthusiastic, after researching his legacy and deeply troubling past. Many of the Nicaraguans with whom I conversed had also lost much of their fervor for Ortega and the Sandinistas. Ortega had taken over full control of the party, scrapped presidential term limits and successfully brought all legislative branches, the police force and practically all government ministries under his control. In Nicaragua if you aren't with the Sandinistas, you're against them. To get a job as a teacher or with any government agency, you need to be a vocal Sandinista supporter or at least hide your discontent for the party.

After starting a master's degree in the autumn of 2015, I dropped out a few months into the program when I was offered a job with a US-based NGO to work in experiential education in Nicaragua. A few months later I moved to Nicaragua, and with the exception of a few visits to friends and family abroad and a three month stint in Costa Rica, I started to live there permanently. Nicaragua had become my home. It was my happy place, the place where I had grown so much both personally and professionally. I had decided in December 2017 that I wanted to make a life for myself in Nicaragua. Being an enthusiast of this country, I knew that during my time there, there would most likely be some sort of upheaval, be it a natural disaster or political uncertainty—these events were all too common in the history of the largest Central American nation. In spite of this premonition, like many in Nicaragua, I never believed it would happen in April 2018. I had expected that any political upheaval would follow the death of Daniel Ortega, now aged 73 and rumored to be very sick with lupus.

"Come on Juan, hurry up, we're always late!" I shouted to my good friend whom I had been staying with for a few days in the city of Masaya.

"Calm down, give me a chance, I'll be five more minutes!" He quipped back at me.

We're always late, I thought. *I'm always late.* I had a bad reputation of being late to everything, much to the amusement of my Nicaraguan friends who would joke that this Scot was more Nica than British, taking Latino time or as we called it, *la hora Nica,* to a whole new extreme. Not wanting to be late to the start of the Mother's Day March in honor of the mothers who had lost their children during the protests in late April and early May, I yelled again to Juan to hurry up. Juan, his two nephews and I were going to drive to Managua, the chaotic capital of Nicaragua, located about forty minutes from the city of Masaya. We clambered into my tiny 4x4 Jimny, all dressed in blue and white, the colors of the Nicaraguan flag. I felt a mixture of emotions: apprehension, excitement, sadness and stress. I knew very well that it was illegal to participate in a protest as non-Nicaraguan citizen and I had also seen the brutality with which the police had responded to the protests over the previous 6 weeks.

"Tranquilo," calm down, Juan said, patting me on the back to reassure me.

"My mum and dad are going to march on my dad's motorbike, and my two nephews are coming with us. This is a peaceful march, it's Mother's Day. There's going to be lots of women, men and children—nothing bad is going to happen!"

Juan had a good point, but I had seen too many scenes of violence first hand over the past 6 weeks and had been bombarded on Whatsapp and Facebook with news articles and photos of the horror of the violence employed by the Ortega regime to feel fully calm. I had promised my mum back home that I wouldn't participate in any protests, but I had also had enough of seeing this government massacre its citizens, who I now felt were my kin. I figured that there would be hundreds of thousands of people at the march and so in spite of my height and pasty white skin I wouldn't stand out too much.

Ever the planner and organizer, and in charge of safety and security for the NGO I worked for, I turned to Freddy and Dennis, Juan's nephews who were aged 15 and 13 and stated firmly:

"Listen, you are coming with me, I am responsible for your safety. If shit goes down and things turn bad, you do what I say and don't make any attempts to disobey me! Got it? I don't want to sound dramatic but we need to have a plan in case things turn violent."

"Got it!" replied Freddy immediately. "Got it!" said Dennis nodding his head as he admired the placard that he had spent hours crafting.

We set off from Masaya at 2:45 pm. The march was due to start at 2 pm but given Nica time and our tendency to be late, we left late and soon hit the traffic on the *Carretera Masaya,* the highway that connected Masaya and Managua. Luckily, I knew this route well as I frequented it a few times a week for work, so I was able to veer us off down some less congested back roads. During the times of standstill, there was a defiant atmosphere, with most of the passengers in cars, trucks and buses waving the blue and white Nicaraguan flag out of the windows in solidarity for those who had been murdered by the blood red and staunch black Sandinistas.

The political situation in Nicaragua had become somewhat lethargic over the past few years. With no credible opposition, along with Daniel Ortega's consolidation of power, elections at all levels brought the same results—a sweeping majority for the Sandinistas. In 2016, Daniel Ortega won his fourth term as President of Nicaragua and his Vice President running mate was his wife. Yes you heard that right, his wife Rosario Murillo. Many claim that Daniel Ortega wants to create a new family dynasty in

Nicaragua and due to his illness, he is setting things up nicely for his wife to take over. I remember driving around Managua on Election Day 2017. My friends and I laughed as we heard the results of the municipal elections come in over the radio. Every major city on the Pacific coast, where the majority of Nicaraguans live, saw landslide victories for the Sandinistas. Overall they gained 73% of the votes—to no one's surprise.

The events that led up to the current Nicaraguan political crisis have been in motion since 2013, but there were two events in April 2018 that led the Nicaraguan people to say enough is enough, to come out in their masses and continue to protest. The first of these began on April 3rd 2018 when forest fires broke out in the protected nature reserve *Indio Maíz* and burned for over 10 days, destroying over 5,500 hectares of the reserve. The government claimed that a farmer was responsible for the blaze but many have refuted this and claimed that it was the government who started the fire strategically to destroy forest in the area where they were planning to build an interoceanic canal. This forest fire and the government's response to it led to many taking to the streets of Managua to protest.

Then on the morning of April 18th 2018, the Nicaraguan government officially announced the reforms to the country's social security system, *el INSS*, which would lead to employees paying 0.75% more on their salaries as contributions, employers paying 3.5% more in contributions for their employees, and retirees would have to contribute 5% of their pension to *el INSS*. The social security system in Nicaragua has a huge deficit but people were outraged as they viewed government spending and mismanagement of *INSS* funds as the root cause of this deficit. People were angry, as the government had spent their money on elaborate constructions that remain empty and contracts had been given to Daniel Ortega's cronies. Moreover, Daniel Ortega's children and family members had gained control over many of the country's industries: buying up malls, hotels and a petroleum company, to name a few. The imposition of social security reforms due to Ortega's mismanagement of funds was the straw that broke the camel's back.

On the evening of April 18th, Nicaraguan citizens both young and old took to the streets to exercise their human and constitutional rights: freedom of speech and freedom to protest. Ortega's government had a long history of quashing protests. That night was no exception. These protests occurred in Managua and in six other cities across the country. On this first night of protests the government sent its paramilitary youth wing, *la Juventud Sandinista,* to enter the crowds of protesters and violently attack them. This led to the riot police, *los antimotines,* responding with grave violence against the protesters. On this first night of protests no one was killed but several people were injured. The government's plan to quash the resistance had been successful—or so they wrongfully believed.

With the spread of information on social media platforms, the disturbing photos of government forces brutalizing unarmed innocent protesters outraged people throughout the country. The following day, on Thursday the 19th of

April 2018, thousands took to the streets across the nation to protest against the government. Enough was enough; the people were tired of the abuse of the Ortega-Murillo government.

Over the course of the weekend, Daniel Ortega addressed the nation twice; on the second address he repealed the *INSS* reforms that had caused the initial protesting. During this weekend though, police and paramilitary forces used deadly violence against protesters and by April 23rd, at least 27 people had been brutally murdered by state forces. Hundreds more had been injured or arrested.

Having taken the back roads, we arrived at the mall *Galerias Santo Domingo* in Managua and found a place to park. We got out of the car, applied sunscreen, as it was a typical blistering hot day, and went to the supermarket to buy some water and snacks. We then walked about 30 meters to the Jean Paul Genie roundabout, the starting point of the march. For kilometers ahead of us, all that could be seen was a sea of blue and white. Flags flying high, in protest of a government that had by this point massacred 91 innocent Nicaraguans. The streets were crammed. As we began the 4 kilometer walk towards the Central American University, *la UCA,* where the march was due to finish, the atmosphere did not feel as tense as I had imagined. There was a tone of defiance in the air, of camaraderie as the hundreds of thousands of people marched down one of Managua's main highways.

As we progressed down the highway, I saw the somber faces of many Nicaraguans, young and old, tearing up at times as they remembered those who had been killed by the state. There were occasional vehicles moving down the streets alongside protesters. Patriotic Nicaraguan music boomed, people held placards with anti-government slogans, and mourners dressed in black carried photos of the fallen. About one kilometer down the road, we met up with Juan's parents who had arrived on his dad's motorbike.

I have seen protests in the UK and the US, some of which had turned violent, but this protest was completely peaceful. Some youths wielded mortar cannons, and would shoot them in the air on occasion to send an insolent signal to the government that their violence will not quiet the people.

I was in continual contact with friends who were somewhere in the march and those protesting in other cities throughout the country. When we arrived to the Plaza de las Victorias, about one kilometer from the endpoint, we saw several protesters who had climbed up the statue of the celebrated national boxing hero Alexis Argüello. We paused here for about ten minutes. I spoke to Juan's mum while Freddy went over to climb the statue, taking with him the placard made by his younger brother. I took some photographs of Freddy and of other protesters. I felt emotionally overwhelmed; a combination of sadness and joy. Sadness that the place I called home was being tormented brutally and that so many innocent people had lost their lives. Joy that the people of Nicaragua were standing up to a dictator and demanding their freedoms and a change in government.

We continued about 100 meters further when we met up with our friend Giovanni who had just come from work. As we stood in front of the Hilton Princess hotel on the *Avenida Union Europea,* the crowd fell silent momentarily. Then all of a sudden thousands of people surrounding me broke into song, singing a very somber version of the Nicaraguan national anthem, *Salve a ti, Nicaragua*—Hail to thee, Nicaragua. In this moment I was moved to tears. The haunting beauty of hearing this anthem on this day, one that commemorated those who had been murdered, was impactful to say the least. After the anthem finished, Juan's parents said goodbye and headed off back to Masaya on their motorbike.

Roughly, 10 minutes later as we continued down the highway, some 700 hundred meters away from the finishing point, a huge amount of commotion began. Hundreds of young people, some armed with mortar cannons and others completely unarmed, starting running towards *la UCA.*

"What's going on? Why are all those young guys and girls running towards *la UCA* with mortars?" Juan looked panicked.

"Let's go and see!" added Giovanni.

"No, let's not!" I said. "Obviously there is something bad happening, most likely the police or paramilitary are responding to the protesters with violence! Listen Juan if you want to go, I can't stop you, you're an adult, the same applies to you Giovanni. But I'm taking Freddy and Dennis with me and we're getting the hell out of here!"

"*Calmáte*, chill out. Don't be so dramatic," responded Giovanni.

"*Tranquilo,* I'm not going to go either," responded Juan.

"Dramatic? Listen, both of you are my friends and I care deeply about you and I also want to support the cause and get rid of this son of a bitch Ortega. But what good is heading into a violent and chaotic situation going to do? We are unarmed and untrained in how to use guns and the government has heavily armed police who shoot to kill. I'm not going to be another martyr to the cause. We can all do far more alive!"

"Okay, okay," replied Giovanni, "Let's go, my car is not parked too far from here, we can all go and then I can drop you off at your car."

We were all in a state of disbelief and confusion as we hurried along one of the side streets towards where Giovanni's car was parked. Upon arriving at the car, which was located a ten-minute walk from where we left the march, I took out my phone and saw that I had 8 missed calls from 3 different friends. I tried to call David, José and Erik back frantically—unable to get through to any of them. All three of them had been in the march and had started off earlier than we had, so I was deeply concerned for their wellbeing. My phone was at 1% battery and as I tried to redial David, my phone turned off. Without any way of charging it, I resigned myself to the feeling of helplessness that overcame me.

The 25-minute drive to where my car was parked at the mall felt like hours. Not knowing fully what had happened at *la UCA,* coupled with having no idea if my friends were safe plagued my mind. Giovanni, Juan and his nephews began receiving messages about the deaths and injuries that had occurred in front of *la UCA.* There were rumors that the government had stationed snipers on the nearby baseball stadium and had calculatedly killed some protestors and that police and paramilitary had injured more people. I lived about 3 blocks behind *la UCA,* and so after hearing the news of this brutal violence and still being unsure of the gravity of the situation, Juan and Giovanni convinced me that I should stay the night in Masaya.

Upon entering my car, I plugged in my phone and we got ready to set off to Masaya. As soon as my phone turned on, I frantically dialed David's number. No answer. *Shit,* I thought. I immediately tried Erik—no answer. *Fuck.* Then I called José, as his phone rang out, I started to imagine the worst. *Could my friends have been killed or injured? Where are they? Are they in the hospital? Should I go look for them?* As his phone was about to ring out, José picked up and shouted at me frantically:

"Are you okay? Is Juan and everyone else okay? Where are you guys?"

"We're all okay" I responded, "We're about to head back to Masaya. Are you okay, are Erik and David okay?"

"Yeah we're fine, we just got back to my place," replied José. "Things have gone crazy. Do not come back to Managua tonight."

José explained that he, David and Erik were at *la UCA* when people started screaming and they heard gunshots. Before waiting around to see what was going on, the three of them ran towards the alleyway at the side of *la UCA*, and kept running without looking back. Four blocks later, they arrived at his house, only a block away from mine.

"Thank God you're all okay!" I said. "What the fuck happened?"

"We had just got to the end of the march when everyone started screaming and running towards the main gates of *la UCA,*" José said. "We could hear gunshots, it was madness."

I thanked him for the information and for checking in on us. I was sweating profusely—the air conditioning in my car was broken and I was consumed with stress and anxiety. After my call with José, I felt somewhat relieved. With one fewer concern plaguing my mind, my priority became getting myself, Juan, Freddy and Dennis out of Managua and back to their home in Masaya.

That car ride took about 1 hour and 20 minutes because of the traffic—many protesters were returning south to their hometowns and cities. That hour and 20 minutes were tense and silent. Occasionally, Freddy would update me on information he was receiving on Whatsapp. Juan was glued to his phone: to Facebook, Twitter and Whatsapp, getting information and checking in on all of his friends. As we arrived back to their house in Masaya, I dropped everyone off and drove around the corner with Freddy to park my car in a neighbor's driveway. When we got into Juan's house, all of his family members were crowded around the TV watching *100% Noticias,* one of the only non-state funded news channels. We heard from the reports that in Managua there were 4 confirmed deaths and over 20 confirmed injuries.

That night I laid on the spare mattress in Juan's room. In spite of being exhausted from walking in the heat and using up my adrenalin supplies, I could not fall asleep. I kept thinking about the events of the day and what had just happened. I cried a little. I was so overcome with anger and frustration. I had just been to the march where everyone was peaceful. This march was to commemorate the 91 people who had already been killed—how dare Daniel Ortega murder more innocent civilians! My rage was soon replaced by a haunting feeling of luck. If it hadn't been for our tardiness, we would have been at *la UCA* when the shooting started. I started to think of the worst-case scenario. I was thinking that me being so tall and white, I would have stood out amongst the crowd and would have been an easy target for a sniper. Goosebumps consumed me. Finally at 3 am I feel asleep.

When I awoke the next morning, May 31st, for a split second I thought that the events of yesterday had all been a nightmare. This image did not last long. Upon entering the living room of Juan's house, I heard the news. *100% Noticias* reported that at least 15 had been killed in protests across the country and close to 200 hundred more had been injured. Later the death toll rose to 19 and there were reports that the government had issued orders of shoot-to-kill and that snipers had pointedly shot protestors in fatal areas of the body. Six weeks into the protests and the death toll was now over 100. Mother's Day 2018 will forever be in the history books of Nicaragua; another day where the brutal forces of Daniel Ortega and Rosario Murillo's dictatorship massacred innocent Nicaraguan civilians.

By the end of June, the death toll had neared 400. The government became less overtly violent, but the next wave came which was mass arrests, with so-called enemies of the state being kidnapped from their homes and workplaces and being hauled off to jail, sometimes without a formal charge. People were arrested for giving water to those who manned the barricades and roadblocks. On my way to and from Masaya and Managua, I had my car searched by heavily armed police who were looking for people bringing arms or supplies to anyone who opposed the government. On one occasion an armed officer asked to see my mobile phone, to check my social media. Posting anti-government material was enough to be taken away to prison. Luckily for me I don't have Facebook downloaded on my phone.

My contract was about to end with the NGO and I was almost certain they would pull out of Nicaragua due to the crisis. I had been job hunting since April and swiftly ramped up my search. Everywhere I applied to, both schools and NGOs told me the same thing—we think you're a great candidate but we can't hire you at the moment due to the situation. With things becoming less and less secure each day and my prospects of finding employment dwindling, I decided to start applying to jobs elsewhere and I began mentally preparing myself to leave Nicaragua, to leave the country held hostage by a monster.

A Monster Lives Here

He tricked you with his talk of equality,
He played on your desperation and exploited your poverty,
He took the credit for the blood, sweat and tears of others.

He painted himself as the liberator—standing up to the dictator and the force of Uncle Sam,
He couldn't accept when you chose his opponent to rule,
He abandoned all of his beliefs to regain power at all costs,
He used and abused your women's bodies for political and personal gain.

He stole from you,
He lied to you.

Now his forces murder, torture, rape and traumatize you!

Nicaragua, a monster lives here,
This monster must be ousted
This monster's forces need to go.

Stay strong Nicaragua ... The monster will never win!

THE NEW NORMAL
CARLOS LUNA LEÓN

In loving memory of Donald Espinoza.

It was the first time that Eric and I were in a hotel but slept in different beds. The discussion had reached an impasse last night when the heat of our drinks emboldened our positions and we began to yell at each other in the middle of the bar. We got back to the room at nine, interrupting an evening that was meant to be unforgettable, and turning it into a battle that reminded us again of the reality: that our relationship had ended and that no piece of it was salvageable.

I take refuge in my phone, and he takes refuge in his. From his bed, he breaks the silence by saying that the worst thing that had ever happened to him was having met me. *There is no need to exaggerate, surely worse things will happen to him*, I reflect. I let him talk, and in my head I promise myself to never resurrect a relationship as senseless as this one.

Eric continues threatening to never see me again, saying that the next day he will return to the city on his own. He turns off the light and gets ready for bed. I turn the light back on, since I will need it to read the book that I had found in my backpack. He is obviously annoyed at me having done this, and his annoyance fills me with delight. If he wants to be upset, I will give him real reasons.

The book is *A Moveable Feast*, by Ernest Hemingway, in which he recounts his daily life in Paris and his relationship with the great artists of that time. It was clear that Woody Allen based his movie *Midnight in Paris* on this book and for that reason, I found it marvelous. One sentence truly struck me, and I wrote it down in my notebook, following the advice that I had read in a list meant to help authors experiencing writer's block: "Write down good quotes from other authors." I liked the entire paragraph, which was a quote that Hemingway attributed to Gertrude Stein:

"The main thing is that the act male homosexuals commit is ugly and repugnant and afterwards they are disgusted with themselves. They drink and take drugs, to palliate this, but they are disgusted with the act and they are always changing partners and cannot be really happy."

I don't take this too seriously; I am well aware that Ernest was a misogynist and a homophobe, but in a way it seems like he was right. It was impossible for me not to reflect upon the relationships that I had had over the past ten years. I had left behind the closeted men for the ephemeral.

I set aside the book and that idea lingers in my head. Once again, I turn off the light and I sleep hugging my pillow. Eric hugs his and begins to snore. At five in the morning, I wake up and go to the bathroom. As I look in the mirror, it feels like I am still dreaming; I notice all the specks of gray which have been appearing in my hair. I approach Eric's bed and he seems distant, even while asleep. I want to throw myself at his side, entangle my legs with his and sleep with him for a few hours, but I contain myself and return to my own bed.

I wake up again at eight. By now, Eric is already awake. We don't speak, not even to say good morning. I slip on my shoes and a clean shirt, and leave the room to walk around the city by myself. I make the obligatory stop in front of the cathedral where Rubén Darío was laid to rest. I light a cigarette and I spend a while at a cafe called *El Sesteo*. Despite my lack of appetite, I order breakfast and eat merely to have the energy to take the wheel of the car and continue my trip, which had been painstakingly planned with travel schedules, expected arrival times and a special playlist.

We had decided to take this trip while sitting in a restaurant in Managua, where we had planned to talk about "us." We arrived in León yesterday afternoon, after a relaxing drive on the highway, during which we held hands and listened to music.

León, the former capital of the country, surprised us with its desolate streets. The hotels had locked up their entrances, many well-known businesses had closed, and the best restaurant in the city had been burned after the flames spread from the CUUN student union building, which rather than being a center of legitimate student resistance, was yet another "autonomous" institution manipulated and utilized as an arm of power by the presidential couple. Such desolation fills even the most indifferent individuals with despair. It was logical that many years would need to pass before the country would resume the path that it had taken before the crisis.

As we searched for a hotel near the city center, the transformation of León was apparent. In spite of the naive individuals who dogmatically claim that the country has returned to normality, the truth is that the streets of cities such as León are filled with mourning, and numb pedestrians with dumbfounded expressions. The city and its lethargy feels like a bubble in which time has stopped. The place we found was called *La Posada de Doña Blanca,* where they told us that they do not accept credit cards, only cash.

The last time that we were in the city was for Holy Week, only a few weeks prior to the 18th of April. I remember that occasion clearly: we stayed in a hostel with a view of the cathedral. At midnight we walked the streets of the city center and the central park, feeling safe—so safe that we lit up a joint in the street. Eric climbed up one of the lion statues around the cathedral and a sudden feeling of paranoia gripped me when one of the security guards, whom I mistook for police, approached us and told us to put out the joint and even dared to check our pockets.

We then walked a few blocks toward a gay club located in the city center. The place was called Go Bar. It was empty, save for four couples who in the clandestinity of the dimly lit room kissed and danced. Eric is an excellent dancer. Cheerful, fawning and attentive, he always seemed ready to say positive things about me. He was a first-class flatterer. He has thick eyebrows and brown eyes, a well-kept beard and dark skin. In Go Bar, they wouldn't stop looking at us, me disheveled and graying. Being thirty seemed more fun with Eric. He had that spirit of a traveler and an adventurer. León was always our favorite place to escape.

We couldn't stop laughing once we got back to the hotel. We tumbled into the same bed and made love until our exhaustion put us to sleep. The air conditioning unit made a strange noise and dripped all night. When we awoke, the bed was surrounded by a puddle of water.

The truth is that investments and tourism in Nicaragua were just beginning to bud. On long weekends, the more privileged residents of the capital would routinely leave Managua for the northern mountains, Pacific beaches or the Pueblos Blancos. I knew this to be true, as I work in a travel agency that partially closed its operations in June. Now our Nicaraguan clients, who used to be interested in visiting Somoto Canyon or the Island of Ometepe, are instead in the market for travel packages to go to our neighboring countries and obtain American visas. It seems like everyone wants to flee. Since April, nothing has been normal in Nicaragua. State terrorism, some call it. Coup violence, claim others.

"It is all a political movement! Even the bishops are Twitter politicians that incite hate!" claimed Eric.

When I met Eric, I knew he worked for the Attorney General's office, but I never thought he was a proud, disciplined Sandinista militant. And I, not belonging to any political party, quickly came to oppose the government when the first protests were brutally attacked. I went to every march and every protest, I shared news on social media. It was impossible for me not to be indignant with the disturbing images that appeared on my phone, so I took to the streets that for eleven years have been dominated by this regime.

Eric, relentlessly loyal to the party, started to defend the National Police and their repressive measures, alleging that everything was a plot concocted by the imperial Americans and the Sandinista Renovation Movement (MRS). For a moment, I thought that he would put himself on the right side of history, that he would join me at one of the marches, that he would resign from the Attorney General's office and that he would not be complicit in the jailing of innocent people accused of terrorism. But, then again, I thought that our relationship would last forever.

Things became unbearable. His own family was against the government; they wanted him to leave the job that they had been so proud of before, but that now they were ashamed of. A family full of life-long Sandinista militants who, like many, have come to condemn the actions of Ortega-Murillo and their followers.

Eric and I became disrespectful to the point of screaming at each other in public. After that, we agreed not to see each other until things calmed down.

But things did not calm down quickly. April gave way to more protests, *tranques* in the cities, rallies, fires, looting, persecutions, national strikes, student rebellions, and civil disobedience. Eric and I became more distant for a few weeks and it was only the nostalgia that we felt for each other that brought us back together. We made the decision to not discuss politics, and to not be a couple. Just friends. This treaty seemed reasonable to me, and we began to see each other every two weeks. This trip to León was a natural consequence of wanting to be together.

The elegant colonial city has been a witness to the violent protests from the beginning and has experienced ongoing arrests of students for organizing anti-government protests. The same happened to youths in Granada, Masaya and Managua, in a raid that imprisoned over fifty people in just one weekend. Self-organized citizens who called themselves the "*azul y blanco*" held rallies outside of police stations to demand the liberation of the political prisoners, who were expressly taken to the cells of El Chipote in Managua, where the government locked up everyone they accused of terrorism.

I finish my breakfast and slowly return to the hotel. I walk down the street with the hostel where we had stayed during Holy Week, and I can't help but remember that incredible night and our subsequent getaway to the nearby beaches of Las Peñitas where our bodies became one beneath the bright light of the moon.

Everything about those nights was different from the current reality in which Eric threatened to return to Managua on his own. I was doubting whether or not he would go through with his promise, but upon returning to our hotel, I watched him get into a taxi and disappear down the hot, dusty road. I light another cigarette before going back into the room, and I smoke it calmly and thoughtfully. Smoking cigarettes makes me feel a physical discomfort which matches my internal conflict. As soon as I enter the room, I fall into bed.

Long before our political differences manifested themselves, in the nearly two years we spent together, we felt the natural wear that all relationships experience. Jealousy, character incompatibility, and loss of sexual chemistry. Perhaps one decides to take a long look at himself, ignore the differences, convince himself that relationships take time, that they aren't always good, and that it takes work to maintain a relationship. On the other hand, the arguments between Eric and I became too constant, and finally the inevitable occurred. But after you end a relationship, second chances are common. Some of these encounters are brief, while others result in another few years. Ours would last one week.

As I pull the car out of the hotel parking lot, I hit another car which was parked outside. Without stopping to see the damage, I speed out of León. I notice half-burnt billboards of the presidential couple. The city was still recovering from Sunday's raid and the pro-government paramilitary attack in which they shot at protesters outside of León's police station. I decide to take the old highway to Managua, since it is less trafficked. Going 100 kilometers per hour, I listen to songs from the nineties and I smoke every half hour.

I often feel that there is nothing better than solo travel. It helps me forget the worst parts of the weekend and clear my mind. I see *tomatierras* along the suburban highway approaching Managua. They have already set up electricity in their settlements and they proudly display the red and black flags of the Sandinista Party. These *tomatierras* are Sandinista agents who have illegally invaded, occupied, and seized over 11,800 acres of privately owned land, affecting millionaire investments and areas of production. Neither the police nor judges have done anything to help the affected landowners, because those affected are opponents of the regime.

"The Commander stays because he stays!" they sing and dance at the government's rallies, held at public universities. The Nicaraguan government forces all public school teachers to follow the Sandinista doctrine and attend these pro-government events. These state institutions have also asked their employees to sign letters condemning the evil coup terrorists. In the bar in León, I asked Eric if the government believed that those coerced signatures, along with the sentencing of mostly innocent people, would be enough to contain the damage and convince the international community and the public opinion of their farce.

"We have all been instructed not to incite hate on social media. It is better to leave that to the miniscule people on the Right!" he answered.

And this was the problem for many. This made-up Sandinista reality could sometimes create convincing illusions of stability and freedom. For a long time the government seemed well-intentioned, though bureaucratic—and it was clear that many officials embezzled public funds. It was like a romantic relationship that had to end. Although it hurt, it was for the best.

Both heads of state and romantic partners should be replaced periodically, leaving power and their comfort zones. Kick them out. Let them rob others of their money and time, but not the same people for eternity.

"So why is everything normal then?" asked Eric. "The people want a return to normality; they want to work and travel. It affects you directly, yet you don't realize that you should be promoting peace on your social media. Maybe if you did, you'd have more business at the travel agency."

"Don't worry about my job. You already have a lot on your plate, helping convict innocents."

"Innocents that held the cities hostage with *tranques* for three months?!" scoffed Eric.

"Have you forgotten why they had to put up the *tranques* in the first place?"

The reality is that at the beginning of the protests barricades (*tranques*) were raised to stop the bullets of the riot police who shot at protesters. The barricades were also raised on each block to stop Hilux trucks filled with paramilitaries from entering neighborhoods, looting private businesses, and burning public buildings as a false flag operation meant to defame and delegitimize the protesters.

"Well the *tranques* have been taken down, thank God."

"Thank God? No. Thanks to those who came to tear them down with force and mercilessly kill the people they encountered."

"And you think that those people were unarmed?" Eric retorted. "Do you truly believe the photo of the dead man with a slingshot in his hand? They had firearms and after they were killed, their comrades took the guns away and staged the photos of the corpses holding a slingshot or a mortar. But yes, in reality they were armed."

I keep driving and Eric's incongruous words keep running through my mind. I don't want to stay in Managua. I keep driving and finally I arrive at the Masaya volcano. I stopped for a while to appreciate the scenery at a viewpoint with a restaurant called *La Vista del Ángel*. It starts to rain as soon as I get out of the car and I get mud all over my feet and sandals. I go straight to the bathroom to clean myself up and dry off, then I order a coffee to warm up.

The rain didn't last long and once it cleared up, the views of the volcano and its rocky, green valley filled me with tranquility. There is nothing better than nature to calm one's self.

I check my phone. It's four in the afternoon. No new messages from Eric have arrived. I didn't know if he had made it home safely, but I thought it imprudent to call him or inquire about his whereabouts. I opened Whatsapp and I saw that he was online, so he must be safe. He probably went to the courts where they were holding the trial against the two young *costeños*[13] from Bluefields accused of killing the journalist Ángel Gahona during the first few days of the protests.

It disgusts me that Eric is part of this corrupt system, and that he's truly convinced that the crisis was caused by a failed coup d'état. The government propaganda claims that they won, and that the participants in the "coup" have been defeated. They accuse anyone who tells the truth of being biased against the government.

As much as I wanted to, I couldn't inquire into Eric's participation in the case against the two *costeño* men from Bluefields. I have always been particularly interested in them. It was one of the most famous cases, along with the killing of the 15 year old Álvaro Conrado, who was shot in the neck, presumably by a sniper, while bringing water and

---

[13] A person from the Caribbean coast of Nicaragua.

provisions to the protesters around the cathedral in Managua. Witnesses affirm that he was taken to the hospital where he was denied medical attention, by the direct order of the Minister of Health. He bled out and died upon arrival at a different medical center.

"That is another lie. If it were a sniper, they would have split his head open. And nobody denied him medical attention. It is all a lie. It wasn't even his parents who took him to the hospital. They have been influenced by hearsay. The protesters were the ones who let him die. They probably needed martyrs for the revolution, though this is not even a revolution. They don't have an ideology, they don't have real sentiments. They are being manipulated and deceived by all the money being sent to them. It is all because they want a coup d'état."

Very well then, I thought. Those who govern this country are not even a political party. They are an ideological sect and a criminal terrorist organization. There's not even a true council, they don't let anyone advise them. It is just the two of them who govern, and nobody else. A coup d'état is the least that the couple deserves.

"So have you not seen the progress in this country?" asked Eric.

"And have you not seen the installation of a family dynasty? His wife is the vice president! His successor!"

I hadn't argued this much with Eric since the 21st of April, when the presidential couple gave their first pronouncement in front of the cameras of their state-owned media channels, alongside representatives of the army and the police, to strategically impose fear.

"It's just that they're not the type of politicians who come out and talk nicely!" excused Eric.

"Of course not! They're politicians who send people to kill you if you protest against them in the streets!"

What the entire country expected in that first pronouncement was for the president and his wife to accept blame, to call for a return to law and order, and to arrest the police officers who had disobeyed their orders. Nobody expected for them to wash their hands of any responsibility so brazenly. Not once did they mention the students who had been killed for their cause.

"Because all of them were killed by the Right!" insisted Eric. "The police acted too gently for my liking. Many deaths could have been avoided if the police had restored order. I don't understand how someone as intelligent as you cannot open his mind. All of this is a charade put up and financed by the United States. Just like the Americans want to occupy Venezuela to steal their oil, they wish to destabilize Nicaragua to control our most valuable resource. They want to control our interoceanic canal project."

Another farce, I told myself. The idea of the interoceanic canal is just a smokescreen to expropriate the land of thousands of poor farmers and sell the wood from the forests.

"You should listen to the advice of my colleague and work towards eliminating the hate in this country… Everything you guys feel for us is hate. You resent that this country has progressed and that it is thanks to us. You believe everything you see on television and social media. Open your eyes."

I light the last cigarette in the pack. I break the menthol capsule with my teeth and breathe in as much smoke as possible to make myself feel dizzy. I decide to linger in the restaurant until the late afternoon, when the volcano's summit starts to glow with a dense, reddish tone from the exposed lava in its crater. The quantity of lava had increased greatly in the past few years and it became a tourist attraction for both national and international visitors, who used to arrive daily and wait in long lines along the highway for their chance to see the spectacle. Why is there such beauty in an imminent disaster?

My phone rings and my heart skips a beat, thinking that it is him. Upon checking it, I see that it is just one on my Whatsapp groups in which my sister had shared the latest news:

#BreakingNews: Orteguista judge declares the two youths Brandon Lovo and Glen Slate guilty of murder, accused by the government of killing the journalist Ángel Gahona, on April 21st in Bluefields, while the reporter was livestreaming the confrontations between police and protesters. The judgement was made behind closed doors and

access to the courtroom was only granted to journalists working for the regime's propaganda outlets.

"At this rate, our country will soon be on par with sub-Saharan Africa!" I write in the group chat, before setting aside my phone. It was impossible for me not to look for Eric in the photo of the courtroom. Was he part of the prosecution in this case? It made no difference; I knew that even if he weren't part of this specific case, he would undoubtedly be part of some other case against innocent protesters.

In court, Brandon and Glen were photographed smiling. The image quickly went viral, and it became an example of maintaining dignity in the face of absurdity, and the act of smiling in front of the cameras when being arrested has been imitated by other political prisoners.

Upon returning to the office the next day, I felt rejuvenated. The trip down the highway made me feel well again, and the absence of the lawyer made me feel even better. I helped two clients, who purchased a travel package to obtain their American visas in Panama. Aside from those fleeing, nobody can afford to travel.

Almost all of my colleagues were laid off. The owner of the agency had been very clear in his opposition to the government and he participated in all of the marches with a megaphone in hand, calling for an indefinite national strike. It didn't take long for the army to accuse him of some crime, and for the police to try to arrest him at his home, though this plan was interrupted by his neighbors who refused entrance to the police cars, forcing them to retreat.

"With all certainty, the police are going to come looking for me. I need you to manage the business for a few weeks," he informed me.

There isn't much for me to manage though. I put on some loud music and browse social media, mostly Twitter. The photos of the students captured in León went viral, among those arrested was a trans student. They were going to form part of the over 300 people accused of organized crime for participating in the protests. This was a new phase in the crisis: persecution and punishment of the protesters.

That same day, the Nicaraguan government would receive another international condemnation in the form of the UN report: "Repression and retaliation against protesters continue in Nicaragua, while the world looks away," claimed Zeid Ra'ad Al Hussein, the United Nations High Commissioner for Human Rights, just before leaving his office, and being succeeded by the former Chilean president Michelle Bachelet.

Upon leaving work I encounter a Sandinista demonstration, an event which had been convened by the government. I arrive home and open a bottle of vodka, first pouring myself a drink on the rocks, then another with a splash of cranberry. I look at my phone, and I still have no new messages, other than a few notifications from my group chats, discussing the president and his wife, who proudly presented 500,000 signatures demanding the condemnation and prosecution of the "coup terrorists." Considering there are over four million Nicaraguans of voting age, this represents a shameful minority, especially considering that the government refers to the opposition as "*minúsculos*[14]," without mentioning that the majority of those signatures were from state employees who, under threat of being fired, were forced to write their names. With all certainty, Eric's name was there. Even if he weren't forced, he would have signed it with pleasure.

As I pour myself a third drink, I hear a knock on my door. It was as if I had summoned him.

I let him in and avoid making eye contact. "Congratulations on the sentencing of the two *costeños*!"

I have no desire of being neutral with him; I am certain of his direct participation in the sentencing of protesters, and I have no doubt that he was standing in the plaza, listening to the Sandinista rhetoric at the demonstration that I had passed earlier. They quickly rejected the UN's report, calling the defenders of human rights liars. They went as far as to ask the Costa Rican government for the list of over 25,000 Nicaraguan refugees in their country, in order

---

[14] A term repeatedly used by Vice President Rosario Murillo to refer to the opposition as a minority of insignificant or minuscule individuals. This term has been utilized ironically by hundreds of thousands of anti-government protesters to highlight that the true minority in Nicaragua are those who continue to support the Ortega-Murillo government.

to extradite and prosecute those who are awaiting "Nicaraguan justice," two words which when put together made no sense whatsoever. There would be no justice until Daniel Ortega and Rosario Murillo leave the country—or die.

"I didn't come here to fight with you!"

He was dressed in black pants and a long sleeved shirt. I couldn't help but notice the briefcase that he brought with him, containing countless legal cases. I used to be so proud of Eric's passion for his work. Before April, I thought he was a professional lawyer, enamored with his work.

It seemed like he wanted to tell me something and when he began to explain, I froze.

"I am going to be the prosecutor in the case of the students who were captured in León. I am willing to show you the evidence," he said, boasting his briefcase. "Whatever it takes to make you see that I am not imprisoning innocent people. They killed a student, burned the CUUN, and kidnapped militants."

"Is this how you want to convince me that there's a way to mend our relationship? Eric, stop playing with fire. Stop accepting tainted money, and stop trying to get me back. I am not going to be with you, ideologically or romantically. You made sure of that yourself."

"I am telling you that there is strong evidence, and you're incapable of being humble and opening your mind?"

"How many years in prison will you give the *costeños*?"

"Twenty-three, minimum."

"And by me opening my mind, will you release them? You know that they're innocent."

"Only because *100% Noticias*[15] says so?"

"Along with the international community, the wife of the victim, the expert witnesses, the Inter-American Commission on Human Rights, the UN…"

"They'll leave tomorrow…" he murmured between clenched teeth.

"Who will leave tomorrow?" I asked, confused.

He showed me a text message from his colleague who said that the next day the Chancellor of the Republic of Nicaragua would ask the UN human rights representatives to leave the country.

"They're being expelled from the country, and you're proud of that?" I said with my mouth agape.

---

[15] An anti-Ortega news source that continues to transmit stories condemning the government—despite its temporary suspension from national airwaves in April, and the government's continuous attempts to silence their reporting.

"They are not being expelled. They were here to be part of the National Dialogue to remove the *tranques,* and now that there are no more *tranques* and everything is normal, there is no reason for them to be here."

"Oh, so the UN representatives were going around with the masked paramilitaries 'liberating' the *tranques* and using excessive, criminal force?"

After that, I had nothing else to add.

"Well if the UN is leaving the country tomorrow, you can leave my house today!"

"Whatever you say… but it is you who should stop playing with fire," he said while pointing his finger at me. "Stop supporting the plot of secret, conspiring politicians who want to overthrow our government. We've already planned it all out: soon we will prove that the NGOs were involved in the attempted coup. We've already assembled the case against those who were teaching workshops on 'Democracy,' 'Leadership,' and 'Networking.'"

"Of course! Because the problem was education, right?"

I asked him for his copy of my house key, just to annoy him. Yet another ephemeral man has left my life, leaving me with a sense of relief and nostalgia. I would find another man, one who was not enslaved to a defunct ideology. At the end of the day, new things are always more exciting, and if the path were open for Nicaragua to condemn the regime for their crimes against humanity, it was also open for me to rid myself of toxic relationships.

And the words of Hemingway come back to my mind, and I reflect on everything that I will have to drink and consume to rid myself of the disgust I feel for having once been with such a corrupt, ephemeral man.

TO THE COMMON BUREAUCRAT EVAN DAUS

People tell me to turn my hate into love.
But how?
My chest: heavy with animosity,
More than I thought I could possess
The Orteguistas have always been inept
But now I see their villainous ways.

Ortega was never a true governor,
He and his companions crave the slaughter
Like jaguars who have been starved for 23 years.
They've found an excuse
To resume their homicidal hobby.

Ortega may be a pile of shit on a fresh white bed
But his putrid filth has seeped into all of the sheets below.
Even educators, sworn to serve our youth
Have seized the unrest to double down on their allegiance to the
party.

Was the promotion worth it?
You have forsaken your own people.
You will not receive the forgiveness of God.

Ortega and Murillo clutch power because theirs is absolute.
But to the common bureaucrat,
To the neighborhood policewoman,
How do you sleep at night, knowing exactly whom you serve?
Every Nicaraguan knows the struggle of making ends meet,
But you have lost the moral north by chasing a paycheck.

I wish I could forgive a few of you.
Maybe if I could see your point of view,
Then I could let go of this thick, palpable hatred.
I've not found any redemption for you.

Violeta Chamorro and Dr King have done it;
They are the alchemists who transmute hate into love.
One day I might discover their ways
But long and arduous will be the path,
Before I finally may bury this dark albatross.

THE PATH FORWARD
EVAN DAUS

Over the past twenty years, Nicaragua's democracy has eroded and power has become concentrated in the office of the presidency. During this period, Daniel Ortega used his influence to lower the percentage of the vote necessary to be elected president from 45% to 35%, allowing him to win the 2006 election. Once in power, he eliminated presidential term limits, paving the way for his third and fourth terms. He dissolved two opposing political parties: the Sandinista Renovation Movement (MRS) and the Conservative Party of Nicaragua (PCN), disqualifying them from participating in elections. Under Ortega's rule, the Supreme Court of Nicaragua has granted the president far-reaching powers, including the appointment of the heads of both the National Police and the military.

Although there are currently no longer weekly massacres in Nicaragua, the crisis has evolved into a new phase. The government officials, paramilitaries and police who are responsible for the violence have not been charged with any crimes. Instead, hundreds of peaceful protesters have been taken as political prisoners and have been charged with terrorism. As grave as the current political situation is in Nicaragua, we must look forward and identify ways to restore true democracy in the country and prevent future crises.

I believe that to accomplish this, Nicaragua will need to change several aspects of its government: decentralize power, instate checks and balances, eliminate clientelism and nepotism in hiring, audit the use of public funds, hold corrupt politicians accountable for their crimes, and allow international observation of their elections.

In the immediate future, most Nicaraguans support advancing elections to 2019, although Ortega has stated that he will not consider this measure. The majority of Nicaraguans also support having their elections overseen by international organizations to prevent manipulation.

I would advise that all levels of the Nicaraguan government reassess their hiring standards. It is common for Nicaraguan state employees to belong to the ruling party, and a change in administration usually precipitates the firing of all previous employees and the rehire of employees loyal to the new administration. This trend handicaps the efficacy of public institutions and is detrimental to the common good.

Historically, corrupt politicians in Nicaragua have not been punished for their crimes because all members of the

Nicaraguan National Assembly are immune from prosecution. This policy clearly does not serve the interest of the public, and should be eliminated.

Moreover, I believe that the powers of the president should be reduced, and term limits should be reinstated. The Supreme Court of Nicaragua and the National Assembly should serve as checks to the president's power, rather than extension of it, as has been the case under Ortega's regime.

Lastly, I encourage all foreign powers to impose economic and diplomatic sanctions on Ortega and the Nicaraguan government in light of their human rights abuses. Nicaragua is a small nation and is vulnerable to international sanctions, so this pressure could be effective in removing Ortega from power. The international community should also be ready to provide support to Nicaragua in rebuilding their democracy when the time comes.

Nicaragua is experiencing a dark chapter in its history, but the corrupt, self-interested officials are outnumbered by ambitious and constructive Nicaraguans who want to improve their country. Progress does not come easily and all of us need to take a stand against human rights abuses and the degradation of our freedom.

The crisis in Nicaragua is humanitarian in nature, and as humans we all have a responsibility to act. I encourage you to do your own research on the current Nicaraguan crisis, and I implore you to discuss what is happening with your friends, colleagues and elected officials.

This crisis cannot be ignored. It will not be forgotten.

ABOUT THE ANTHOLOGIST

Evan Daus served as a Peace Corps Volunteer in Nicaragua until a humanitarian crisis forced his evacuation in April, 2018. Daus is an author of short stories and poetry, and has plans to release a full length novel.

Made in the USA
San Bernardino, CA
06 April 2019